WINNING AT WORK AND CRUSHING IT AT HOME

Work-Life Harmony

For Female Leaders

DONNA MARIE COZINE, ED.D.

DEDICATION

This book is dedicated to the thousands of female leaders who serve so brilliantly. You are amazing. You are valued. You are loved. You are a blessing. I see you!

In Friendship, Love, Leadership, and Sisterhood,

DMC

Sister Leader Press

Fairport, NY USA

Copyright © Donna Marie Cozine 2024

Published 2024

DISCLAIMER

Editor: Donna Marie Cozine, Ed.D.

Photo Credit: Sue Zeccola

Cover Design: Donna Marie Cozine, Ed.D.

ADVANCE PRAISE

Donna Marie's support has been instrumental in my growth as a leader.

> Dr. Toyia Wilson
> Assistant Superintendent

The fact that she's a female leaders is Why I went to her specifically because it's different Being a female leader.

> Leticia Oseguera
> Superintendent

Donna Marie individualizes her mentorship and Coaching for your particular abilities, strengths, and needs. She has a lasting impact on the leader and the Leader's ability to spread that to her staff.

> Jacqueline Simpson
> Superintendent

As a female leader there were some things I needed to address and resolve. She gave me the Confidence to tackle those challenges in my life.

> Kelly Bonde
> Principal

Working with DMC has been a great game changer. I'm connecting with a person who knows what the struggles I am having as a female leader. She pushes me to think in different ways, work in different ways and to do better each time I met with her. She is passionate about helping female leaders think bigger, stronger, and differently.

Dr. Saundra Russell-Smith
Director of Family Engagement

Working with Donna Marie has helped me in more ways than I could even begin to say. She has helped me mentally and physically be a better leader. I am very thankful for the work we did together.

Liza Jacobs
Principal

Dr. Cozine is solutions oriented which has Helped me become a solutions-oriented leader too.

Rhiannon Tobeck,
Director of Arts and Technology

One of the best decisions I made for myself As a leader is to work with Donna Marie.

Ruth Tolbert
Assistant Principal

Donna Marie really helped me Through a period of burnout.
Dr. Tamara Wallace
Director of Special Services

Donna Marie is a constant source of support for me as a female leader.

Tracy Y. Harris
Director, Career and Technical Education

TABLE OF CONTENTS

CHAPTER 1: You Are Wonder Woman... Literally..............1

CHAPTER 2: We Do It Differently 9

CHAPTER 3: The Self Care Leadership Syllabus 17

CHAPTER 4: The Leadership Appreciation Syllabus....... 53

CHAPTER 5: The Leadership Systems Syllabus................77

CHAPTER 6: The Wonder Woman Within You—Living the
Life You Deserve 105

ABOUT THE AUTHOR..111

FOREWORD

I love it when things come together just right. It happened when I first heard Dr. Donna Marie Cozine speak about work-life harmony for women. She was presenting at a Roundtable at the American Association of School Administrators' Annual Conference. Her session title "Work Life Harmony for Female Leaders" drew me in.

She was just like the rest of us: a knowledgeable, dedicated educational leader, and she was speaking about real work and life experiences. She had figured it out! Donna expertly shared practical strategies to support a work/life balance. I knew then I wanted her to tell her story to our Indiana women in leadership.

The work Donna shared with us is written within the pages of this helpful guide. Readers will find themselves picking it up over and over again, putting the ideas into practice to feel better, lead with a purpose, and experience positive outcomes. I'm sure you will get as much out of it as the Women in Indiana have!

Jane Rogers
Retired Superintendent
Milan Community School Corporation

Milan, Indiana
WELL Coordinator
(Women Educators Leading Learning)
IAPSS
(Indiana Association of Public School Superintendents)

CHAPTER 1

You Are Wonder Woman… Literally

"Who you are surrounded by often determines who you become."

—Vicky Saunders.

In a world where women are often expected to do it all lead the boardroom meeting, manage the science fair project, navigate a fitness routine, prepare dinner, and still find time to be an attentive spouse or partner it's easy to feel stretched thin, overwhelmed, and occasionally defeated. Let's pause for a moment. Take a deep breath and reflect on this truth: You are Wonder Woman… literally. Not in the "perfectly polished Amazon warrior princess" kind of way, but in the real, resilient, and resourceful way that makes you a force of nature at home and at work.

If you're reading this, chances are you're striving to harmonize the demands of your career with the responsibilities and joys of home life. You're a leader— whether that leadership is evident in the workplace, in your family, or in both realms. Let's face it, sometimes it feels impossible to do everything well without sacrificing something. That's where this book comes in. You're not alone, and more importantly, you don't have to choose between winning at work and crushing it at home. The secret lies in *work-life harmony*—not balance.

The Myth of Balance vs. The Reality of Harmony

The term "work-life balance" often feels like a trap. It paints a picture of an even scale where work is on one side, life on the other, and your job is to make both sides weigh exactly the same. Let's be real, life doesn't work that way. Some weeks are work-heavy, filled with deadlines, strategy sessions, and projects. Other weeks might demand more of your attention at home a sick child, a milestone anniversary, or just the need to recharge with your family.

Harmony, on the other hand, acknowledges that these priorities shift. It allows for flexibility while still ensuring that both areas thrive. Think of it like a symphony where different instruments come forward at different times, but they work together to create beautiful music. By learning how to prioritize, delegate, and focus on what truly matters, you can lead that symphony with confidence.

What Makes You Wonder Woman?

Let's take a closer look at what makes you extraordinary. Like Wonder Woman, you embody courage, strength, and a deep desire to make the world better. Instead of a golden lasso though, you've got a smartphone loaded with back-to-back meetings, grocery lists, and reminders to pick up dry cleaning. Instead of a magic tiara, you wield your ability to multitask, lead with empathy, and adapt under pressure.

The truth is even Wonder Woman has her limits. Behind the superhero persona, there's a person with fears, doubts, and the need for support. That's why it's critical to invest in yourself—not just as a leader, but as a woman who deserves self-care, boundaries, and systems that sustain her.

This book is your roadmap to becoming a real-life Wonder Woman, grounded in *empowered leadership* and *work-life harmony*. Together, we'll explore how to:

- Create and enforce **boundaries** to protect your time and energy.

- Develop systems that make you more **efficient** and less stressed.

- Focus on **priorities** so you're not just busy—you're effective.

The Foundation: Self-Care Isn't Selfish

Let's start with a foundational truth: self-care is not selfish. It's survival. Too often, women feel guilty for prioritizing their own needs. They think, *If I spend time on myself, I'm taking it away from my family or my work*. The reality is that you can't pour from an empty cup. Taking care of your mental, physical, and emotional health isn't a luxury—it's a necessity.

Consider these questions:

- When was the last time you did something just for you?

- How often do you get adequate sleep, exercise, or time to reflect?

- Do you allow yourself moments of joy without feeling like you need to justify them?

If your answers are vague or filled with qualifiers, it's time to shift your mindset. Think of self-care as recharging your battery. When your energy is full, you show up as a better leader, partner, and mother. You think more clearly, manage stress more effectively, and make decisions with confidence.

Boundaries: The Armor You Need

One of Wonder Woman's most iconic traits is her indestructible armor. For you, that armor is your boundaries. Without them, it's easy to become a victim of burnout, resentment, or chaos. Boundaries protect your time, energy, and well-being.

Here's how to create and maintain them:

1. **Get Clear on Your Priorities:** Know what matters most in your life right now. Use this clarity to decide what gets your "yes" and what earns your "no."

2. **Communicate Your Limits:** Be assertive yet kind when setting boundaries. For example, "I'm not

available for calls after 6 PM because that's family time. Let's reconnect tomorrow."

3. **Hold Yourself Accountable:** Boundaries only work if you respect them yourself. If you've set a rule about not working on weekends, stick to it.

Priorities: The Compass for Your Choices

It's tempting to try to do it all. But just because you *can* do something doesn't mean you *should*. Wonder Woman knows when to wield her strength and when to step back. Similarly, focusing on your priorities ensures that you're putting your energy where it counts.

Ask yourself:

- What are my top three priorities at work and at home right now?

- Are my actions aligned with those priorities?

- What tasks or commitments can I let go of to create more space for what matters?

This clarity allows you to show up fully in both your professional and personal life. It's not about doing more it's about doing what matters most.

Systems: Your Secret Weapon

Wonder Woman has her gadgets, and you have your systems. These are the tools, habits, and routines that make your life run smoothly. Systems are the antidote to overwhelm. They free up your mental space, reduce decision fatigue, and allow you to focus on what truly matters.

For example:

- **Morning Routines:** Start your day with intention. Whether it's 10 minutes of journaling, a quick workout, or simply drinking coffee in silence, a consistent morning ritual sets the tone for the day.

- **Time Blocking:** Schedule your priorities, not just your tasks. Block off time for deep work, family activities, and even rest. Treat these blocks as non-negotiable.

- **Delegation:** Let go of the myth that you have to do everything yourself. Delegate at work, involve your family in household responsibilities, and outsource tasks when possible. Remember, leadership isn't about doing everything it's about empowering others to contribute.

The Sister Leader Movement: You're Not Alone

As you journey through this book, remember that you are part of a larger movement of women redefining leadership and success. The *Sister Leader Movement* is about creating a ripple effect. When you thrive, you inspire others to do the same. When you model work-life harmony, you empower other women to believe it's possible.

A Final Word: Yes, You Can

You ARE Wonder Woman—not because you're perfect, but because you're powerful. You have the courage to lead, the wisdom to prioritize, and the heart to create a life of meaning and joy. Winning at work and crushing it at home isn't about having it all—it's about having what matters most to *you*.

By the end of this book, you'll have the tools, mindset, and confidence to achieve work-life harmony on your terms. So, fasten your metaphorical lasso and step into your power. Your best life, the one where you truly win at work and crush it at home is waiting and you are more than ready.

CHAPTER 2

We Do It Differently

"Don't follow the crowd, let the crowd follow you"

—Margaret Thatcher

Female leaders bring a unique perspective, skill set, and purpose to the leadership. As a female leader, we just do things differently. Not better, worse...just differently. We have full time responsibilities at work as well as at home. Even when female leaders have the most supportive partners, we still have responsibilities that fall squarely on our shoulders. There are many industries in which women lead. I am using education as a benchmark to show the trends. In the US only 28.5% of Superintendents, the highest leadership role in a school district, are women. The COVID pandemic impacted female leaders more so than their male counterparts. As female leaders left the upper ranks of education 51% of those positions were filled by men, widening the gap. Unless we start doing thing things differently in the way we train and support female leaders the number who leave leadership will grow and the number who move up the ranks of leadership in all industries will shrink.

When I was new to leadership, I was unmarried and had no children. Even then I had trouble with work life balance. I couldn't "not do work" all the time. Because I didn't have external demands on me, I didn't realize how unhealthy it was. I just kept grinding. Fast forward 7 years when I founded and was the CEO of a charter school. I was married and had two children, my son was 2 and daughter 4. My daughter attended the school that I founded, and it felt like all I did was work. Again, I just kept grinding and didn't pause to consider the impact this was having on my family.

One day my husband made sure I understood just what my workaholic, go all day and all-night attitude was costing me. "We didn't sign up for this," he said. As I had my face in my laptop and was working nonstop, I distractedly answered "sign up for what? A credit card?" "No, this life, the kids and I didn't sign up for you to be working all the time and not being present." This was the proverbial slap upside my head. I sat up and thought I better listen!

We began talking about how my lack of being present was impacting my husband and children. I realized then and there that I needed to make some changes. The man who supported me in everything I did was calling me out and you know what? He was right. I vowed that night to change. From the time I got home until the kids went to bed, I was present. Unfortunately, my change ended there. As soon as they went to bed, I was back at it, laptop on my lap and face in my computer. Again, my husband reeled me back to reality. He told me that the changes I made were great for the kids but that I still wasn't present for him because as soon as they were asleep, I went back to workaholic mode. I realized that I had to do better and vowed to make sure not only my children, but my marriage was going to be a priority. I began researching how I could have better work life harmony and changed the way I worked. Here's the issue, there was no one solution, I had to sort through ideas and strategies to create a comprehensive solution.

I don't know about you, but they didn't teach this in my graduate school studies. I also didn't learn it in any support I received from my supervisors. Although many organizations have leadership develop programs, they don't address the additional issues that women face when trying to balance their work and home responsibilities. My life positively changed because of the efforts I made, and I want to share them with female leaders across the world so they too can have the work-life harmony that they deserve. The families who deserve the BEST of them is only getting the REST of them and that needs to change!

The work life balance paradox: it's a contradiction but is terminology regularly used in conversation. Can you have balance between your work and balance in your life? Would you want those two things to be equal?

I'm going to introduce a topic or a terminology that I want you to consider: work life harmony. So here is our reality. As women, we have two full time jobs, the proverbial nine to five, which for those of us in leadership is more like seven a.m. to seven p.m, and then we have the other shift, seven p.m. to seven a.m. We want to be able to go home and shut off work stress and just immerse ourselves with our families. Our wants are simple, we want peace and tranquility and for most of us, sadly, we don't have that. I know I did not have that in the beginning and the reason I didn't have in the beginning was because I didn't know how to do it. I learned how to navigate the realities faced by female leaders and now I feel blessed to help women learn how to do the same.

I have been talking work life balance for a while, and I recently thought it's really balance we are looking for but harmony. Quite frankly, if I need to give more attention to one thing over the other, it better be my family. What's more important to your family? Or your job? Your family? So, what I have been thinking about lately and talking to women about is this idea of the two things living together and complementing each other. What does work life harmony look like to you? For me it looks like not having to answer the phone at 10 o'clock at night because people stopped calling me with issues, it looks like taking my children to their after-school activities without worrying about work, it looks like enjoying watching my son play baseball. Focus on harmony and your family won't be stuck with an overwhelmed and exhausted mother and partner or spouse.

Truth be told I think work life balance is a bit of a misnomer. Most people feel their families should be weighted more heavily than their work but the way they function is in direct conflict with that belief. I prefer to think of it as work life harmony or work life symbiosis. In this way work and life can peacefully coexist without one taking away from the other. As female leaders we are constantly distributing our energy between work and life and, like a tightrope walker, we consistently try to not fall off the rope that is our lifeline.

For many female leaders we constantly feel pulled between our home responsibilities, and our work responsibilities. We feel pulled between being good enough at home being good enough at work. We worry that we're not giving our families and our organizations what they need from us. This constant pull is just exhausting. One night I had a board meeting, my daughter Juliet was in the first grade. The board meetings were at 6pm and she refused to go home. I had two choices: force my 5-year-old to go home or take her to the meeting with me. I chose the latter.

At that board meeting, Juliet sat on my lap, and I participated in the board meeting as I always did. At the time it just had to be that way. I not only started the school, but my children attended the school. There were many times where my children were at events at which other CEOs of organizations wouldn't have their kids but for me, that's what I needed to do to make it work. I wasn't going to force Juliet into a car and force her to go home and be upset. It wasn't worth it.

The Merriam-Webster definition of balance is an even distribution of weight enabling someone or something to remain upright and steady. When we achieve balance, it means all things are equal. Well, here's the paradox of work life balance. Do you want your work and your life to be equal? Do you want the importance of your work and the importance of your life to be the same? Herein lies one of the issues in America. We don't work to live. We live to work. If you look at our counterparts in other countries, they don't live to work. They work so that they can live the lifestyle that they want. We don't do that. We work and work and work and then work some more. It's this puritanical work ethic that as Americans, we pride ourselves on. In reality this is making us unhappy and, in some cases, sick. I want you to rethink this idea of work life balance and I want you to think of the word harmony. Harmony is the quality of forming a pleasing and consistent whole. This is what we should strive for.

I've spoken with hundreds of women who have consistently identified feeling the same because of the demands of their jobs and their families. They are consistently overwhelmed and exhausted, feel unappreciated and taken advantage of, and feel like they have too much work and not enough time. If you're reading this and wondering "Why does that matter?" Well, let me tell you why.

Your happiness is important,
your family is important, and
your wellness is important.

My goal is to help you stop dreaming about work, spend more time with your family, and finally live the life you deserve! To do this we'll solve the 3 biggest problems that stop female leaders from **Winning at Work and Crushing it At Home** once and for all: not having a focus on self-care, having undefined boundaries, and priority misalignment. Preventing burnout for female leaders is possible. The following chapters will provide you proven strategies which will enable you to **Win at Work and Crush it At Home** for good.

Journal Reflection:

- What does "winning at work" look like to or mean for you?

- What does "crushing it at home" look like to or mean for you?

- Do you feel like you have work-life harmony right now? Why/why not

CHAPTER 3

The Self Care Leadership Syllabus

"If your actions create a legacy that inspires others to dream more, learn more, do more, and become more, then you are an excellent leader."

—Dolly Parton

When I talk about self-care with leaders there definitely is a trend. The women who are the most stressed out and feeling like they are NOT Winning at Work NOR are they Crushing it At Home respond with some variation of "I don't have time for self-care" or "Self-Care? What's that?" It's obvious that self-care plays a significant role in a person's happiness, satisfaction, and ability to have the best life ever. Why then do women not take time for themselves? I was recently in a therapy session and my son was waiting in the waiting room. He knocked on the door and came in and asked for help with his homework. I said "Ok, bring it in here and I'll help you." The therapist said "We're going to try something here. Theo, mom is not going to help you right now. Go out there and move on to another question that you can answer. You didn't do anything wrong, but your mom needs to focus on her right now." Theo shrugged and left. The therapist said "You need to stop dropping everything for them. You've trained them that whatever they need supersedes what you need."

Newsflash!!!! This is exactly what I would tell a client yet here I was slipping back into behaviors that didn't serve me. I think it is common for women to put the needs of everyone else before their own. I think of my Irish Grandmother who died at 75 of a totally curable cancer because she hadn't been to the doctor for 35 years. She made sure everyone else had their needs taken care of but why not her own?

When those who these women love need something they make it happen.

- My child needs a tutor? Here's a check.

- My son wants to play on a travel baseball team? Where do I sign up?

- My husband doesn't play enough golf? Here is a gift certificate for 18 holes.

- My parents need to go to a doctor's appointment? Let me drop everything and take them.

BUT.....

- I need to focus on my wellness, $39 a month is too much for a gym membership!

Wait? What?

The foundation of **Winning at Work and Crushing it at Home** is taking care of you. The first line of defense is Self-Care. The goal of the Self-Care Leadership Syllabus is to help you solve the problem of feeling overwhelmed and exhausted all the time. The biggest issue most female leaders have is that they don't address their own needs. They focus all their energy and resources on everyone else. The steps in this section will help you focus on YOU and what you need to become refreshed and energized.

Your Mission Matters

All leaders need to determine what type of leader they want to be and in what capacity. What many fail to realize is that so much of this depends on where you are in your life. As your life changes your priorities change and so too will your leadership mission.

When I started in leadership, I aspired to being a superintendent of a school district. I was 100% on that track and was the heir apparent in the district in which I was a principal. The superintendent was pouring into me to be sure that when he retired, I would be ready to step in and take over. All of that changed when I met and decided to marry my husband. In an instant my desires for my future turned on a dime. Some people questioned my decision to leave my position and move to a totally different community, but I never did. For me it was more important to marry this amazing man and start a family than it was to stay where I was and climb the leadership ladder. We've been married 17 years and the fulfillment of all my dreams came from that decision.

As female leaders we often navigate a web of responsibilities and expectations. This constant negotiation occurs while we try to not burn out. In order to avoid burnout, the first thing female leaders need to do is to determine their mission. In my first book *So, You Want to Be a Superintendent? Become the Leader You Were Meant to Be* I devoted an entire chapter to this topic because it is THE most important thing a leader needs to figure out. Defining and understanding your mission as a female leader is critical to your success. When you are clear on your mission you can steer your way through the many tasks, crises, and obstacles that present themselves in your daily leadership walk.

A person's mission can change and that is totally natural. Discovering our mission is not a static process, and vice versa, rather it is always evolving. As our mission's change so to do our lives. This ability to pivot in response to a change in your mission reflects your adaptability and responsiveness to the one constant in our lives: change. Figuring out your mission and ensuring you are living it is the first step in Winning at Work and Crushing it At Home. Once you understand your mission and truly live it you can be your authentic self and experience joy. You will embody your purpose every day, it will be reflected in how you make decisions, and how you interact with stakeholders. People will know exactly what you believe, what you stand for, and what you will support (and not support.)

Mission misalignment can be a huge problem for female leaders and can contribute to feeling burned out. This burnout is a manifestation of the continuous stress and exhaustion that is brought on by asking yourself "why am I doing this work?" or "what does it even matter?" Discovering and living your mission provides you a buffer against burnout. When your mission is your guiding light, it provides you a vehicle through which to tackle the many challenges and stressors that inevitably come your way. Being driven by your mission makes those challenges more manageable and less overwhelming.

For female leaders, burnout is a real and present risk. However, by identifying, embracing, and living a mission, aligned with your values and purpose, you can foster resilience and find joy and fulfillment in your leadership role. Remember, your mission is dynamic, and allowing it to evolve with you is key to maintaining alignment and preventing burnout over time. Engage in continuous self-reflection and be ready to adapt your mission as needed, and you'll be well-equipped to lead with passion, purpose, and balance.

Consider my client Simone. Simone and I started to work together midway through the school year. Simone had been leading an elementary school for about 6 years. She had persevered and led her organization through COVID and had emerged from that feeling totally burned out. She felt like she was failing as a principal when she absolutely wasn't. When we began to work through what she thought her mission was she kept coming back to wanting to be a superintendent because that was what for that position that her training had prepared her. When we took the time to unpeel the onion, she determined that being a Superintendent wasn't her ultimate mission. She had to shift her mindset from feeling like being a failure for not having been a superintendent already, to a mindset of celebration because she realized that being a superintendent of a school district was no longer her mission.

She realized that she wanted to serve students and families in a larger way than as a building principal. Together we prepared her for that transition, and she now works for a neighboring school district as a Director of Family Engagement. Not only is she doing work that is totally aligned to her personal mission, but she has less stress and is better compensated! Talk about a win-win. S shared with me that her perspective switched "I now understand that I didn't fail I just outgrew the position (of principal)." This is absolutely true! As leaders we often hold ourselves to extremely high expectations and are really hard on ourselves if we feel we are not meeting them. Instead, we need to hold ourselves to appropriate expectations and reflect and determine the root cause of why we are not feeling successful and address those.

Determining your Mission

To determine your mission, you need to do some deep reflection. With my clients we work through a framework and create personal mission statements. To do this I ask them to reflect on the following questions:

- What are you excited about when you wake up in the morning?
- When you go to bed, what do you wish you had done more of during the day?
- What motivates you to be your best?
- What do you want your legacy to be?
- How can you make the lives of others better?
- If you didn't need to bring home a paycheck, what would you be doing with your time?
- What is currently missing in your life?
- What fulfills you?

Once you work through those questions, and maybe some more that pertain directly to your situation you can create your own personal mission statement. Here are some that my clients have created:

- I want to live a life of joy and laughter. I want to surround myself with positive people and have time to be present with my family.
- I want to rise to the level of superintendent while still having a work-life harmony. I intend to use my gift

of leadership to grow other leaders while still having time to focus on my personal growth.

- I want to leave a legacy of love for my family, my colleagues, and those I serve as an educator.

- I want to provide high quality program for underserved populations.

Burnout is often a manifestation of misalignment between our mission and what we are doing every day. When we spend our time doing things that do not make us happy, fulfill us, or bring us joy, we deplete our energy and enthusiasm for our work. Take time to create your own mission statement and determine if you have alignment. If you don't have alignment, figure out what you need to do differently.

The Importance of Value Alignment

As a female leader, embodying and embracing your core values is critical in being successful at work and satisfied with your life. When your role as a leader is aligned with your core values, you will ensure intrinsic harmony that will enable you to resiliently navigate challenges with clarity and grace. This alignment is your North Star guiding you through all aspects of your day, life, and journey as a leader.

Ensuring this alignment can be done regularly if you focus on it. Reflecting on moments of joy and fulfillment in your life helps ascertain the values that are deeply ingrained in your identity. These values are the foundation of your leadership style, influencing how you interact with others, make decisions, and perceive your role within the organization. Understanding and acknowledging these values is the first step towards aligning your leadership approach with what truly matters to you.

One of my clients, Lisa, realized that she was working in an environment that was not aligned to her values. She wanted to be able to be a leader whose experience was understood and valued by her school district. She had a lot to share with other leaders but, because of the size of the district and its organizational structure, there were no opportunities for her to do that. Although Lisa was highly effective at her position and her school was recognized as a turn-around school under her leadership, she decided to look outside of her district for other opportunities. She now works in a larger district where there will be opportunities for her to continue to grow and help other leaders within the district.

I can remember when Lisa came to the realization that she needed to move on. A sense of resolution and calm came over her. She finally felt like she was able to bring value to her new organization. This change was her own personal Renaissance.

Explore your Values

Think of a time when you were happy, felt fulfilled and looked forward to your next step in life. Next, jot down the answers to these questions:

- What was happening at that time in your life?

- What personal values did you tap into during this time?

- On the other hand, think of a time when you felt down and uninspired and reflect upon the questions below.

- What was happening during this time?

- What was your life missing?

So.... what do you value in a position?

Find Your Core Values

Take the survey to determine your core values: https://posproject.org/character-strength-survey-adults/

Once you know your core values reflect on how you can honor these every day and think about what you are doing that is not honoring those values.

Core Value	How can I honor this value?	What am I doing that is not honoring this value
ex: Honesty	I can work in earnest to be transparent and honest with my stakeholders	I'm not telling the people on my team the "whole story".

Misalignment brings Burn-Out

Misalignment between your values and the organization's culture or expectations can lead to negative outcomes. Misalignment can cause stress and dissatisfaction, the disconnection between what you value and your daily experiences can creat internal conflict. This anxiety can erode your enthusiasm and commitment to your role, leading to burnout and fatigue. This can impede your ability to lead effectively. Leadership demands authenticity, and when you are forced to act against your values, this compromises that authenticity. This disconnect is often obvious to those around you, causing them to question their trust and confidence in your leadership. The gap between your values and those of your organization can hinder your ability to advocate for and implement meaningful change. This can make it very difficult to bring your team together to work toward common goals.

The impact of this misalignment is not only felt at work it is also felt at home. When you spend most of your day engaging in activities that are not aligned to your personal values you are exhausted and often frustrated when you get home. Your patience may very well be running thin, and you may be short tempered with your family. Worse, this constant state of stress can create physical manifestations in your life.

When I was an assistant principal, I worked for one year under an interim principal who did not share my core values. That year was the most challenging of my career. I was ready to quit after working with him for only 4 short months. He treated me subserviently and I did not agree with the way he made decisions or treated the staff I had grown to respect and love over the course of the two prior years. During that year I was physically ill more than I had ever been before. I suffered from migraines, sleep issues, exhaustion, malaise, and depression. I knew this was a manifestation of what was happening at work.

In January I was appointed as a principal in a neighboring school district that would begin in July. I seriously considered leaving in January but chose to stay for the students, their families, and my staff. The misalignment not only caused me to have issues performing my duties at work with grace but it also impacted my home life. I did not have the energy I needed to be regularly present for those who loved and needed me.

Creating Value-Aligned Leadership

Situations and circumstances change in our lives and our professions. If you're feeling as if there is not alignment it is time to work on creating the value-aligned leadership that you deserve. The first step is to regularly reflect on your values. How have they changed, how have you adapted? This regular reflection helps you stay connected with what matters to you thereby helping you to make decision that honor and reflect your true self. Next, you need to spend some time determining fit to your current organization. Understanding if there is alignment between your values and the organizations' culture is critical in enabling you to lead authentically and effectively in that environment. Finally, engage in continuous learning that support your values. This will help your leadership evolve and you will understand how you can be authentic in your leadership journey.

As a female leader, aligning your leadership with your core values is not only essential for your well-being but also pivotal for the success and impact you can have within your organization. Values alignment needs to be a dynamic and ongoing process that requires attention and nurturing. Acknowledging, understanding, and acting upon your values empowers you to lead with authenticity, purpose, and joy, ultimately fostering a work-life balance that is sustainable and fulfilling.

"Why Am I Always so Stressed Out?"

Many women with whom I speak don't understand why they feel so stressed all the time. I know when I was in my "stressed out" stage I couldn't quite put my finger on the why. I was highly competent, well experienced, and well-schooled. I would begin a spiral of self-doubt. "What is wrong with me that I can't figure this out? Instead of realizing that no one ever teaches us how to "do it all" while they do expect us to "do it all." I would beat myself up for not being perfect. I'm not sure why I expected perfection from myself when I consistently showed grace and forgiveness to everyone around me. I was falling into what I call the Perfect Leader Trap, the belief that the leader must do everything, know everything, and be everything to everyone. This perfect leader trap can cause leaders to feel like they aren't doing enough, increase stress levels and cause burnout.

Although stress is an unavoidable impact of leadership. The toll tends to be more multi-faceted and significant for women. Society has put expectations, responsibilities, and pressures upon us that men simply don't have. I always say that as women we have two full time jobs. We have professional obligations during the day and have emotional and domestic obligations to our families as soon as we get home. This system creates an undeniable cycle of stress rooted in the constant balancing act between work and home responsibilities. This chronic stress can also wreak havoc on the physical and mental health of female leaders. Constant and persistent stress causes a myriad of health issues for women. The long-term impact of this constant stress has the potential of jeopardizing their careers, their families, and their overall quality of life.

A stressed leader begets a stressed organization. As leaders our people are looking at us all the time and use us as their barometer to determine if things are good in the organization. It's critical for female leaders to mitigate their stress so that their stress doesn't impact the community within their organization. If they don't mitigate the impact of their daily stress, it can impact the culture of the organization. Understanding and acknowledging the unique stressors faced by female leaders is crucial for creating effective systems that support them and promote a healthier, more balanced approach to leadership and life.

To address the stress that you experience on a regular basis you need to identify stress trigger points at home and at work. When I work with my clients, we spend dedicated time on this process. Not only do we identify the stress trigger points but we create ways to mitigate them. Once we know WHY we are being triggered we can decide HOW we are going to act differently to avoid these triggers. Reflect upon what causes you stress at home and write them down. For me my home stressors are the morning rush, trying to get everyone out of the house and making dinner and getting everyone around the table. Next, reflect upon your work stress trigger points and write them down. For me my work stressors are when staff members don't follow through on commitments and when I can't do my tasks because someone else has not done what they needed to do.

Once you've identified the stress trigger points you need to think about how to plan to avoid those triggers. Write down as many ways as possible that you can mitigate them. Once you've gone through the list pick two or three things to try. For my home stress triggers we packed lunches and book bags the night before, we got up a bit earlier, we had a consistent morning routine, and I set an alarm on my phone which indicates that we needed to start moving toward the car. For my work stressors I created a system to keep the people that I delegated tasks to accountable to their deadlines.

I recently led my coaching group through this exercise and one significant work stressor for one of my sister leaders, a superintendent, was the constant interruptions that happen during the day. We dove down and realized that the reason she was having constant interruptions was because since the organization had been reorganized a system of who people should contact for what topics was never fully rolled out. We created an action plan to ensure these roles and responsibilities were clearly articulated, captured in an artifact, and communicated to all stakeholders. The superintendent planned on implementing some different techniques to organize and block off her time which would also limit interruptions. Voila, many birds...one stone. This is the power of sharing with a coaching group, others may see things that you do not.

Sunday Nights Aren't What They Used to Be

For some leaders Sundays used to be fun days. They were days for watching football and hanging with the family. Sadly, once the stress of work takes over Sunday nights are no longer what they used to be. Sundays start to become a worry session about what the week ahead will entail. This is a common theme with the woman I serve. "Sunday Scaries" or "Sunday Blues" is a reality for many women. This feeling of anxiety can put a pall over the upcoming week, causing more worry for the leader and potentially for their stakeholders. Because of this worry and anxiety, we can lose an entire day with our loved ones, a day we are supposed to be focusing on relaxing and unwinding.

When I was at my most overwhelmed and exhausted stage as a leader my Sundays were terrible. I would wake up and start worrying right away about "everything I needed to do." Sunday night dinner with my family, which should have been fun and relaxed became tense and something I just wanted to get through to get to my work. This was absolutely no way to live. When I started making changes to my life and my work my Sundays got better. I realized that if I just set some time aside on Sunday to "check a few things off my list," I would be able to move on for the day. It is from this experience that I created the Sunday Fun Day Schedule activity with my clients.

To combat the "Sunday Scaries" I work with my clients on a Sunday Fun Day schedule that enables them to have control over how their Sunday and the following week unfold. The schedule isn't rigid but more a loose framework of tasks the leader wants to get done and when those could happen.

Create your Sunday Night Success Plan

Many leaders begin worrying about the workweek on Sunday. This is problematic in many ways. To fight the Sunday worries you will create a Sunday Night Success Plan.

Step 1: List what causes you to have anxiety on Sunday night and brainstorm how you can mitigate the anxiety ex:

Anxiety "Causer"	Possible Mitigation Strategy
I haven't checked my email all weekend	I can feel less stress if I clear my inbox before I go to bed

Step 2: With your family, choose one hour on Sunday that you can set aside to implement your Sunday Night Success Plan.

Record the time here: _____

Step 3: Create your Sunday Night Success Plan

This will be very specific to what cases your anxiety. Use the information from the chart above to schedule

Ex:

5:00-5:15:   Clear my inbox

5:15-5:30:   Write my Monday Musings Email to Staff and Schedule

5:30-6:00:   Pack my bag, make lunches, iron clothes

Beware Imposter Syndrome

Every person in the world has had imposter syndrome at one time or another. Those of us in leadership positions may experience it even more than others. Impostor syndrome is the feeling that you don't belong in the position that you hold. You question your ability to actually "do the thing" that you are trying to do.

I became an assistant principal at 27 and I had a little bit of impostor syndrome in the beginning. When I sat down with teachers who were experienced and had been teaching for way longer than I had I questioned my ability to supervise them. Of course, if I didn't have the ability or knowledge I wouldn't have been there. One thing has become clear as I interact with leaders is that impostor syndrome is real, and it impacts a lot of people. So how can you deal with impostor syndrome? The first thing when dealing with impostor syndrome is to tell yourself that you belong there. You wouldn't have the position if you did not have the chops for the position. Building up your confidence around your ability to hold your position and do the job will help to put impostor syndrome on the bench. I know that's easier said than done. When you're in the middle of an anxious situation or you're struggling with something imposter syndrome is going to come in. To help yourself realize that you are meant to be there, create some sort of a mantra like "I got this" or "I'm meant to be here" or "I'm the woman for the job". A consistent mantra will help you when impostor syndrome rears its ugly head. Whenever I'm faced with a tough obstacle I say, "You've got this DMC" or "You've done harder things than this."

One of my clients, Margaret, was a new supervisor in her school's food service program, it was the first time that she had responsibility over a crew of people. Prior to her being hired one of the team members was taking on supervisory responsibilities. We talked a lot about how she felt like she wasn't the person for the job. We looked at all aspects of her day and identified many times when she was complimented for her acumen. The department that she ran was improving as was the quality of the food which made for happy kids. Even with all the evidence we weren't changing how she felt. She realized that her feelings were emotional and not rational but still couldn't shake it.

I taught her about positive affirmations and suggested that she put post it notes in her office near her workspace with those affirmations. When she felt like she wasn't meant to be there she could have these visual reminders. One day the most amazing thing happened. When she returned to her office there were additional post-it notes written by someone who stopped in her office that said, "You are a blessing." "We are so lucky to have you here." How cool is that? We believe what we tell ourselves so why not tell ourselves how amazing we are? Other people think we are so we should too!

Another technique is to build your confidence is through coaching. When I was the CEO of my school, everyone on my leadership team was offered an executive coach. I had a different executive coach from my team, because my responsibilities were slightly different. My coach was a retired female superintendent, and my staff used a college professor who supported the school leadership team from 2014-2023 when he sadly and unexpectantly passed away. There is a huge benefit to being able to pick up the phone and call someone to get feedback. Often there is no one in your organization in which you can confide. When I became an administrator there was no such thing as coaching for educational leaders and there was definitely no differentiation for female leaders. I was fortunate when I became an administrator because I had my own coach, my mother. When I became an assistant principal, my mother was a principal and soon became an Assistant. Superintendent for Business for a large rural school district in New Jersey. If I had an issue, I could call her and be say, "What do you think about this?" Although her leadership style and mine are slightly different, I benefitted from being able to discuss the issue at hand and how I would handle it or how she had handled it in the past.

Create Your Badass list

Did you know that you are a badass? Yes, you are. I learned a technique from a business coach that I now use with those I coach. Jen Gottlieb taught me something called the Bad Ass list. You sit down and write down all of the things you've done and times you've felt like a Badass. I keep mine in the notes on my phone so I can pull it up as a reminder of who I am and what I've accomplished. I was at a full day in person workshop with female leaders in Indiana.

Recently, I was working with a group of female leaders in Indiana and one of them said. "This last month I looked at my Badass list twice." I said, "That's great and...." She said, "It was just a reminder that I was experiencing impostor syndrome and that I belonged right where I was!"

I was recently working with a client on writing her first book! She had wanted to do her doctoral dissertation on female leadership but was dissuaded from doing so. Although it had been years since she earned her doctorate, she still had a deep desire to write a book about the leadership journey of women. The morning of the writing intensive she shared with me that she thought "Who am I to think I can write a book?" She acknowledged it for what it was, impostor syndrome. As she was preparing to write chapter 2 of her book which was about how she was uniquely qualified to write on this topic I gave her this advice. "I want you to write about you from the perspective of those who love you the most. Those people know that you are amazing and never doubt you. As leaders we often look at every situation from that of a fixer, so we notice what's not perfect, we do the same with ourselves. You ARE THE person who is qualified to write THIS book!" We need to get of our heads about what we perceive are our deficiencies and lean into our assets and truly understand that nobody is perfect.

Imposter syndrome happens to everyone. When it comes for you kick it to the curb using with these strategies. Figure out which strategy will work for you at that time. My wish is for you to see yourself like those who love and believe in you do.

Self-Care is a Necessity not a Nicety

As female leaders we are constantly and simultaneously juggling multiple responsibilities and tasks. When we perceive that all the responsibilities are equally important it is difficult to determine where to start. The relentless pace of our days, the constant responsibilities, the playing "whack-a-mole" when addressing issues and holding ourselves to high expectations can leave us totally drained, both physically and emotionally. I often talk about our energy as female leaders as being a watering can. All day we water our stakeholders, their families, our employees, and our own families. The constant pouring from our "watering can" leaves nothing left for us to pour into ourselves. Regular self-care pours back into our "watering can" and refreshes us so that we can continue doing all the things that only we can do.

"I have too many deadlines to prioritize self-care." is a common objection many of us have heard or even said ourselves: " The truth is, prioritizing self-care is not only important for our overall well-being, but it can actually *help us be more productive and efficient in the long run*. When we're constantly working at a breakneck pace, our bodies and minds can become overworked and overwhelmed. This can lead to burnout, decreased motivation, and even physical illness.

So, how do you make self-care a priority when you feel like you just don't have time? It begins with understanding your unique self-care needs and recognizing that they are specific to you. It's critical to listen attentively to your body and mind, identifying their signals and responding with the care they need. Self-care isn't one-size-fits-all; it's an evolving practice that reflects your changing needs, preferences, and circumstances.

When I work with my clients on self-care plans, I ask them to reflect on the following questions:

- How does your body respond to stress?
- How do you know you are experiencing increased stress?
- What makes you feel better when you are experiencing stress?
- What are your physical needs? emotional? spiritual? nutritional, mental?

Once a client can answer those questions, she can begin to consider what self-care strategies work for her and figure out how to incorporate them into their days and their lives. Creating and adhering to a daily self-care regimen is a powerful proactive strategy. Self-care does not need to be weekend retreats in Bali, although that sounds delightful. Self-care can be small, sustainable practices built into your routine that address your physical, emotional, and spiritual well-being. Whether it's a morning meditation session, a brisk evening walk, a few moments of deep breathing during a hectic day, or engaging with inspirational reading before bed—these cumulative moments of care create a buffer against the inevitable stresses of leadership. Self-care also necessitates you being kind to yourself. Balancing everything is a process, and it is totally okay to make adjustments as you go. It's important to show yourself grace and give yourself permission to make mistakes and learn from them. By practicing self-care, you can find a balance that works for you and helps you thrive in all aspects of your life. I've provided a choice board of simple activities you can use to get started!

Ultimately, it's up to us to prioritize self-care in our lives, even when we're busy. By taking care of ourselves, we can be more effective leaders, colleagues, family members, and friends. Remember, taking time for yourself and your loved ones isn't a luxury; it's a necessity. You are not just educational leaders but also role models for finding balance in life. By embracing these tips, you're setting a powerful example for your family, colleagues, and students alike.

Create your Self-Care Plan

Women who create a self-care plan are more likely to incorporate self-care into their practice than those who do not. Self-care plans should be individualized to the needs of each leader. To create your self-care plan, answer the questions below. A self-care Choice Board is included in this workbook to give you some ideas.

Individual Reflection:
- How does your body respond to stress?

- How do you know you are experiencing increased stress?

- What makes you feel better when you are experiencing stress?

- What are your physical needs? emotional? spiritual? nutritional, mental?

Write down all the ways you can address your self-care based on your individual reflection above. If it is an idea that is something you can do daily indicate that with a (d), if it is something you can do occasionally indicate that with a (o).

Ex: listen to my favorite album (d).... get a professional massage (o)

Create a list of self-care ideas that you can do daily or occasionally. Schedule them into your schedule.

Being Present is Self-Care

Earlier in the book I shared the story of my husband telling me that he and the kids didn't sign up for the life I was giving them. Simply, I was not being present. I hear this concern often when I meet, speak, and work with women across the world. We just feel like we are not there for our families. Even when we are "there" we are not present. My clients and I spend a lot of time talking about being "present". Universally it seems that as women our brains are always processing multiple things at once. We don't give ourselves the time to slow down and process all the stimuli. All of these stimuli coming at as at all times prohibits us from actually being present in the moment. Why is it so difficult to do?

The first step is determining when we find it easy to be present and when we find it difficult to be present. Take a few moments to reflect on the questions below.

- I find it difficult to be present when......
- I find it easy to be present when......

What do you notice? Is there a time of day or a location that lends itself to you being able to be more present in the moment? Are there people who help you stay in the moment? Conversely what is making it difficult.

Next reflect on times when you haven't been present but really wish you were. Was it during a meeting? Family dinner? At a child's sporting event? Capture that below.

- I wish I was more present.......

Finally, in the quiet ask look at all that information and record what helps you be more present. What practices are they? Is it turning your phone to silent? Turning off the computer and packing it in your bag before dinner? Going for a family walk after dinner? Record them below.

The following practices help me be present....

Commit to Being More Present

Now that you've reflected on what is and what you want to be. Complete the commitments below.

I commit to being present:
(when)_____
(how) _____

I commit to being present:

(when)_____

(how) _____

I commit to being present:

(when)_____

(how) _____

Ex. I commit to being present with my family at dinner time by silencing my phone and shutting off my notifications.

I commit to being present with my husband/partner by spending date night on Saturday nights alternating who chooses the activity.

Why Am I Always So Exhausted?

Do you ever feel like you're literally dragging yourself out of bed in the morning and dragging yourself in the door to your house at night? I know this is not the way you want to be. I know it is how I was when I did not have the work-life harmony that I have now. When I present to women's groups a lot of women ask, "why am I always exhausted and more importantly, what can I do about it?" If this is you it is important for you to know that you are not alone. There are many women who go through their life feeling exhausted all the time. Constant exhaustion and not feeling well rested has emotional and medical ramifications. One of my migraine triggers is poor sleep. I know that if I sleep less than 6 hours at night the next day more than likely will be a migraine day. When we don't sleep well enough our systems do not work appropriately. Proper, restful, and restorative sleep is critical.

Exhaustion limits our ability to see and experience the joys that life has to offer. You may see your friends and they have great energy, and you think "what the hell was wrong with me that I just am tired all the time?" If you are a person who is dealing with exhaustion, you need determine the causes and make a plan to address them.

The first thing you need to do is determine if there is a medical reason. If you're exhausted all the time, the first thing you should do is make an appointment with your doctor. Your doctor will most likely give you a physical, check your bloodwork to rule out any medical reason for your exhaustion. Maybe there is a reason you are not sleeping well and need a sleep study to diagnose it. You want to check all those things out to be certain that any medical issues are addressed.

Next you need to look at your current sleep hygiene. There are certain things that you must do before bed to make sure you have a good sleep environment. One of the things that my kids hate is that we don't have televisions in our bedrooms. I read once that the only things people should do in their bedrooms are sleep, get ready for sleep, like reading a book, and being intimate with their partners. Sleep doctors explain that when you enter your room it should send a message to your brain that says, "It's time to sleep." If you enter your room and you watch television for an hour, your brain is not getting the right message. Make sure your room is only dedicated for sleep, getting ready for sleep, and intimacy. It is important that you create a comfortable sleep environment. To do this, you need to have a supportive mattress to your liking, a great pillow, soft sheets and blankets, no ambient light, and the right temperature. These things will be particular to you and if you have a sleeping partner some compromises may need to be made. Staying hydrated and daily exercise also help you achieve restorative sleep. If all the above considerations do not yield positive results, then you need to look at the next possible cause of exhaustion, emotional exhaustion.

Emotional exhaustion is actually very common for those in the helping fields. If we do not buffer our experiences with those in crisis, we can experience compassion fatigue. Compassion fatigue is the result of helping other people through their trauma and stress. It can have a physical, emotion, and even psychological impact. As a leader we can get compassion fatigue from helping our students, their families, and even our staff. Compassion fatigue is more common than you think. Consistent self-care can buffer the impact of compassion fatigue, but the problem is that many female leaders put themselves last thereby not planning self-care practices. Another reason you can be emotionally exhaustion is depression. Depression can be caused by situations, like extreme sadness or it can be a chronic condition.

I can give you an example of situational depression that I experienced. I had three miscarriages before my children.

I remember after my first miscarriage I did not want to get out bed and I was sad all the time. I was confiding in a friend while crying and she said, "If you don't get out of bed now, you are never going to get out of it." She affirmed that what happened was horrible but that I had to keep moving and living. As difficult as it was at the time getting up and moving on with my life was necessary. Maybe you're somebody who has a family history of depression, anxiety, or bipolar disorder. This could be a reason why you are exhausted all the time. Fortunately, we have gotten much more supportive in the US about mental health. You can see your own physician to discuss the potential and/or you can seek assistance through your organization's Employee Assistance Program. Mental health is as important as physical health and if someone has poor mental health it can manifest itself in poor physical health.

Another manifestation of emotional exhaustion is the feeling that "you've just had it!" You may feel like you cannot do another thing today and you cannot continue the grind. Sometimes our emotional exhaustion, which can turn into physiological exhaustion, comes because we're just not working in a way that honors what's important to us. One of the things I talk about a lot, and I work really deeply with my clients on are priorities, boundaries and self-care. Intentionally focusing on all three of those things are going to help you avoid physiological and emotional exhaustion.

Here are some simple things you can do every day to mitigate the impact of stress and limit compassion fatigue and exhaustion. First, take advantage of opportunities to rest your mind. You don't have to be going all day every day. Make sure you eat lunch either with someone or alone but make sure it is an interrupted time of at least 30 minutes. The second is to reduce the amount of sensory input that you're exposed to. Are you in an environment where there's too much going on around you? Shut your door. In the school that I founded we had a CEO suite. People would come in they would chat, make copies, or get a cup of coffee. I would be in my office with the door open, and I would be totally distracted. I was either becoming invested in conversations that were happening outside my office or I would want to jump up and say hello to everybody. If this sounds like you then you must find time during the day to shut your door. Just have some quiet time during your workday. Give yourself breaks from the craziness of the day, take some YOU time. It's okay for you to go for a walk around the building, go outside, check in with your peers, or even take some time to call a trusted friend if you need a little reset.

As leaders we need to be realistic about what is possible to achieve during the day. Think about what is consistent with your boundaries and priorities. What often happens is that we wind up taking on other people's responsibilities because we are not mindful. That load causes mental exhaustion. So be realistic about what you can and should accomplish because some of these things you're doing probably belong to other people. Next, permit yourself to disconnect. One thing I talk about with my clients about is the importance of determining the time when you're done. Maybe you leave the office at 4:30 but everyone knows they can still reach you until 6:00. After that time though you're not going to be checking your emails and you're not checking your work phone unless there's a major emergency. It's okay to "power down" it's going to help calm the mental exhaustion. Finally, the last thing is to make organization a top priority. The more organized you are, the less you're going to become exhausted and overwhelmed. Constantly thinking "where's my stuff" or "what am I doing?" saps your energy.

If you feel exhausted all the time, find out why. Determine if the cause is physiological, emotional, or mental. In some instances, it may be more than just one. Regardless of the cause there is a solution. Speak with a physician, a counselor, or a coach who can help you make some changes that will help you significantly decrease the amount of exhaustion you are experiencing. Once you can do this you can focus on getting a true restful and restorative sleep.

There is a NyQuil commercial with the tagline "Sleep like you did before you had kids." I think that is a powerful statement. I'd like to see my clients sleep like they did before they became stressed out leaders. No longer waking in the middle of the night trying to solve problems, having trouble falling asleep, or having less than restorative sleep because of constant worry. Many women with whom I work cite the lack of restful sleep as a major issue. They wake up with worry about work and are unable to go back to sleep. Some have a fitful night's rest because they are dreaming or having nightmares about work. Some even have trouble falling asleep. Restful sleep is critical for wellness. When we sleep our bodies and minds can slow down and recover from the day's experiences. Proper sleep is essential for physical and mental health. Poor sleep is linked to poor concentration, brain fog, weight gain, and many other negative physical and mental health outcomes. Here are some tips to help you if you are facing some of these issues.

1. **Have a Consistent Bedtime Routine:** Establish a calming bedtime routine. This signals to your body that it's time to wind down.

2. **Create a Comfortable Sleep Environment:** Ensure your bedroom is conducive to sleep. Keep it dark, quiet, and at a comfortable temperature.

3. **Limit Screen Time:** Reduce screen time before bedtime. The blue light from screens can interfere with your ability to fall asleep.

4. **Stay Hydrated (but not too much):** Stay hydrated during the day but try to limit fluids in the evening to avoid nighttime wake-ups.

5. **Practice Relaxation Techniques:** Deep breathing, meditation, or gentle yoga can help calm your mind and prepare your body for sleep.

6. **Be Patient with Yourself:** Remember, it's okay to have sleepless nights. Parenthood comes with its challenges, and it's a journey filled with love and growth.

Sleep Hygiene Survey

Proper sleep hygiene is necessary to get a great restful night of sleep. Take the survey below and then reflect on the follow up questions.

I have a consistent bedtime and routine.
Always   Sometimes   Never

I have a consistent wake up time and routine.
Always   Sometimes   Never

I have a comfortable sleep environment.
Always   Sometimes   Never

I limit screen time 1 hour before bedtime.
Always   Sometimes   Never

I am well hydrated during the day.
Always   Sometimes   Never

I do not drink caffeine after 3:00.
Always   Sometimes   Never

I practice techniques to wind down each night.
Always   Sometimes   Never

I get at least 30 minutes of physical activity each day.
Always   Sometimes   Never

Based on your survey responses create three action steps that you will implement to improve your sleep hygiene.

I commit to:

1._____

2._____

3._____

These basic sleep hygiene routines, if implemented regularly, can help you sleep longer, deeper, and wake up refreshed. What sleep hygiene steps will you commit to tonight to ensure you have restful sleep?

CHAPTER 4

The Leadership Appreciation Syllabus

"Contrary to popular belief, the best way to climb to the top of the ladder is to take others up there with you."

—Maria Eitel

As female leaders we are constantly on the move, physically and mentally. We are constantly juggling many projects, priorities, and people. It's not uncommon to be doing so much that when we finally stop to take a breath, we physically feel like we ran an ultra-marathon and emotionally we feel like no one "sees" all that we've done for them. When speaking with professional leaders I notice that there is a trend, they feel unappreciated both at work and at home. They are used to doing everything for everyone. Eventually when they crash, they not only feel worn out they feel unappreciated.

The purpose of the Leadership Appreciation Syllabus is to address this second major issue female leaders face, feeling unappreciated and taken advantage of. At a recent training I made a statement that some people bristled over. The statement was "If you are being walked all over, it is your fault." I truly believe that if we do not establish and reinforce healthy boundaries, we can't blame others for overstepping them. Creating these boundaries at work and at home is critical in ensuring we aren't feeling unappreciated and taken advantage of.

Healthy Boundaries

When my staff returned to school after schools were reopened during the COVID pandemic I provided a PD session with an anxiety coach for the whole school. The purpose was to learn how to manage our anxiety so we could help children manage their anxiety in the classroom. One of the things she talked about as a self-care technique was making sure that you're setting boundaries and reiterating what they are. Many times, in my leadership journey I have had people overstep my boundaries, sometimes they were my perceived boundaries because I never established them and sometimes, they were boundaries I clearly set. It became my responsibility to hold true to and educate those people about those boundaries. The more transparent and overt we are about communicating our boundaries the less people will overstep and staying in their lane.

The first thing you need to do when checking if people are disrespecting your boundaries is to consider if this person has overstepped in the past. Determine which stakeholder group it was and how your boundaries were disregarded. Are you noticing a pattern? If you are then you should look to yourself first and determine what you can do differently to change that moving forward. If someone is taking advantage of you or making you feel walked all over this is a boundary issue and you are the one responsible for setting your boundaries. Often when someone disrespects our boundaries we get upset, our reptilian brain starts firing and we think "Oh Hell NO!" That is NOT the best time to address the disrespect of your boundaries. You need to speak with the person after you have reflected upon the event, calmed down, and thought out what you are planning to say.

Most times when you address the lack of boundaries you will realize that it was completely unintended. Often, people don't realize that what they are doing is inappropriate and if we think it is then we need to address it. When working with one of my new superintendents we realized that there was a staff member who was very negative toward everything and was testing the superintendent's boundaries almost daily. Prior to this superintendent taking over there had been a half year of an interim and the feelings on the previous superintendent were less than stellar. One day the superintendent called me to talk to me about an email that she had received from this person. The email was totally a boundary breaker. Her initial reaction was to strike back with an email but because we had been talking about how our body responds to stressful stimuli she decided to just pause and call me for advice. Our discussion started with how she felt about this email, how it was way beyond anything he should have sent her and then moved to the idea that there is a pearl of truth in everything. We broke down his complaints to the root cause and looked at that. Taking this avenue allowed us to figure out what the real issue was. The superintendent replied to him when she was calm and asked him for a meeting. At that meeting she explained that she did not appreciate the tone of the email but also realized there was some information in the email that she could address. In handling the situation, she made it clear to the boundary breaker that he was wrong in how he addressed his concerns. Once she reiterated her expectations for professional dialogue the offending boundary breaker was clear that he was wrong in how he handled it and would not address her that way again. She was also able to address the underlying reason for his frustration. This truly was a win-win situation. Now, he tells her all the time how valuable she is to the organization and when he has things that he wants to bring to her attention he does so in an appropriate and professional way.

Setting and Reinforcing Boundaries

It is critical that WE set our boundaries. If we are not clear on our boundaries, then others create those for us. We must be explicit about our boundaries with those with whom we interact and consistently reinforce them. Think of the last time that you felt someone disregarded your boundaries in any part of your life. Answer the questions below.

1. What happened just before?

2. Have you had problems with this person not respecting your boundaries before?

3. If yes, what have you done about it?

4. How did you contribute to this person's ability to disregard your boundaries?

5. Could you have done anything differently that would have avoided this situation

6. How did you follow up with the person?

7. What do you think your next steps should be?

As you reflect upon your answers, you'll be able to determine if you are contributing to your boundaries being disregarded by others. As you are more consistent in your efforts to protect your boundaries you will notice that you will spend less time having to correct people who are taking advantage of you.

- What do you need to STOP doing immediately to create and enforce healthy boundaries?

- What do you need to START doing immediately to create and enforce healthy boundaries?

- What do you want to TRY to create and enforce healthy boundaries?

Now that you've figured out how to protect your boundaries it is important for you to model that for your team. We must lead by example and having a discussion with your team about protecting their times will go a long way to ensure that everyone feels appreciated. Reflect up on the following questions and then discuss them with your team.

1. What times do you think it is appropriate to contact your team?

2. Do those times protect their personal and family time?

3. If it doesn't then pick a better time.

4. How will you contact your team in an emergency?

5. What would constitute an emergency that you may reach out to a team member after those hours?

What commitments will you make to model boundaries for your team.

ex: I will schedule emails that I write in the evening or weekends, so they arrive in my team's inbox during the appropriate times.

Discuss your commitments with your team and seek their feedback. They might add some value around what healthy boundaries look like for them.

Modeling Boundaries for your Family

Once you've established healthy boundaries with your team at work it is a great opportunity to do the same with your family. Involving your family in determining boundaries at home is essential for your family to understand you.

- Have a family meeting and ask each member of your family what activities they feel are essential for you to participate. Then ask if there are any that they don't particularly mind if you miss.

- Share the activities that you feel are critical for you to complete.

- Together make a list of must do and nice to do for both you and your family members.

- Schedule the "must do" activities on your work and personal calendars and highlight them in a specific color.

- Schedule the "nice to do" activities on your work and personal calendars in a different color.

- Do your best to make sure you attend all of the "must do" activities and if possible, attend the "nice to do" activities.

- Repeat the activity monthly or quarterly.

Focus on Organizational Capacity

Often the reason that we feel unappreciated is because we find ourselves doing work that we don't think fall under our areas of responsibilities. Organizations are like living organisms that grow and change. At the beginning of each year and when new people are hired you should take some time with your executive team and board to determine if the way your organization is structured is providing the support that it needs. In the words of Arthur Jones Australian born sociologist and author, "All organizations are perfectly aligned to get the results they get." It is incumbent upon you as a leader to look at the way your organization has been functioning to ensure it is effective.

Step 1: Pull out your organizational chart, hopefully your organization has one.

Step 2: Determine if the organization is following the chart as written.

Step 3: Bring your executive team together and ask them these questions:

    a. Could we be functioning more effectively if we made changes to this chart?

       If yes, then what are their suggestions.

    b. Are there positions that we no longer need or no longer have but are still on this chart?

    c. Are there positions that can be added to this organizational chart to improve our outcomes?

    d. Are there positions that can be combined to improve our outcomes?

    e. Are there positions that can be separated to improve our outcomes?

Step 4: As a team reorganize the chart and create a rationale for the changes.

Step 5: If you are governed by a board present the new organizational chart to them possible adoption. If you are the person who approves changes to the organizational chart, roll it out to the large organization and go live with it.

Clearly Delineated Roles and Responsibilities

In many instances the reason why everyone goes "straight to the top" is because they don't know who else to ask. This contributes to our feelings of overwhelm and the pile of work on our desks. To grow the competencies of your team and protect your time you need to create a clearly delineated roles and responsibilities document to roll out to all your stakeholders. You may choose to have more detailed charts to share with the people who work in your organization and a "Who do I contact?" chart for other stakeholders who interact with your organization.

Step 1: Determine which roles you will be focusing on.

Step 2: Bring your team together and explain the process.

Step 3: Create a shared document where each person can write down their responsibilities. Choose a date by which this will be completed.

Step 4: Bring the team together at the appointed time and look at each person's list. Is everyone in agreement? Be sure to call out situations where the edges may be blurred to see if the responsibilities hold true. Edit your lists as necessary.

Step 5: Create an infographic or chart that makes sense for your organization and is easy to understand.

Step 6: Roll out to your stakeholders. You should roll this out at the beginning of each school year and review it when new team members join.

Develop Relationships that Ensure Mutual Success

So much of our work as leaders is relationship building. We need to build relationships with a variety of stakeholders. Some of these relationships will be positive and some will not. The trick is not spending too much time and mental energy on the relationships that do not yield positive results for your organization or you. Reflect on the questions below and be as specific as possible:

Think of a current relationship that ensures mutual success	Think of a current relationship that does not ensure mutual success
How did this relationship form?	How did this relationship form?
What do you each bring to the table?	What do you each bring to the table?
How do you both act that ensures mutual success?	How are you both acting that does not ensure mutual success?

How do you feel when you interact with this person?	How do you feel when you interact with this person?
Is this relationship necessary? How often do you meet with this person?	Is this relationship necessary? How often do you meet with this person?

After reviewing the chart determine if there is anything that you uncovered from the left column that could be implemented that will improve the right column. Jot those ideas down. Create a plan to either improve the relationship or limit your interactions.

Don't Fear Delegation

One of the things that I find working with my clients is that we often talk about the importance of delegation. Many times, my clients share they are afraid to delegate. There are many reasons why we fear delegation, fortunately there are specific techniques leaders can use to address their fear. These tend to be the four reasons that leaders don't delegate. The first reason that leaders often don't delegate because they fear that the task is it won't get done right. The second one is that we worry that it won't get done in a timely manner. The third one is we say, "Oh, I can just do it really quickly. The fourth reason is that we say, "I'm just I'm not good at delegating."

When I talk about delegation, I liken it to the circus performer who has all the plates, and he/she is trying to balance all of those plates. It makes it very difficult to keep everything up in the air. Unless we're going to clone ourselves or work 365 24/7 There's no way that we can do everything ourselves. It's just not possible. To further illustrate the importance of delegation I offer you this analogy about shoe tying. This is kind of a funny story. I have two children Juliet and Theo. Juliet had occupational therapy which started in kindergarten. I was so panicked that she wasn't going to be able to tie her shoes that we were practicing tying shoes every day. My son didn't have any OT issues and had mostly cool sneakers that had Velcro or the elasticized laces that didn't need to be tied at all. One day when Theo was 10 years old, I realized we never taught him how to tie his shoes. We were tying his shoes before school and double knotting them so they wouldn't come undone. Like a lightning bolt it hit me, I would be tying his shoes forever if he didn't learn how. When we're teaching a child to tie his or her shoe, it's much easier for us to do it for him or her right. It's starts simply enough; we're running out the door because we are always going in a million directions. We say, "Let me just tie your shoe really quickly." In the short term it's a quicker and more efficient but every time we do that, we're prolonging the amount of time that we're going to be tying this kid's shoe. If we continue in this way, we're going to be tying this kid's shoe forever!

It's the same thing with delegation. IF we don't train our people how to do certain things, we're always going to be doing it for them. The other reason delegation is necessary is because we need to grow the people on our teams. So, whether you're a superintendent or principal, there are people who report to you who need to complete their tasks for you to be able to do your job. For instance, if you are doing the district budget and you have 47 schools, you cannot physically go to all those 47 schools and get all their budget information. It would be a full-time job for you, and you wouldn't be able to do anything else. For you to get your budget done it is necessary to delegate to certain tasks to the principals so that they give the building specific budget data a month before the district budget is due.   When we don't delegate tasks like these then we are constantly in the weeds when we need to have a 30,000-foot view.

It Won't Get Done Right

Let me break down the fear that leaders have that the task won't get done right. The first thing we must do is define what done right is. After defining what "done right" looks like you need to explain your expectations. . Next, you're going to gradually release responsibility for the task, and then you're going to monitor progress. One of the phrases that I live by, and I think all leaders should live by is **what isn't monitored isn't done**. It's our responsibility to make sure that we're monitoring people as they're going through whatever task it is that you've delegated to them.

The way that I do things may be different from the way that my assistant does things. Honestly, however at the end of the day, if her method works, it doesn't have to be my method. If you're the type of person that only wants things done your way then you need to check yourself and ask, "Am

I micromanaging?" If you get to that point where you're micromanaging people, that is going to be very difficult for you to delegate because people are never going to want to work with or do things that you delegate because you're hovering over them

To effectively delegate:

> **Step 1:** Define what right is.

> **Step 2:** Outline your expectations.

> **Step 3:** Gradually release responsibility for the task.

> **Step 4:** Monitor progress.

Let me give you an example to demonstrate the process. I delegated kindergarten graduation to my family services coordinator. I wanted certain things, I wanted to make sure that parents were there, and I wanted to make sure that the students had a scholastic experience including them wearing caps and gowns. I didn't care about anything else. This is what "right" looked like to me. I outlined those expectations to my team member and shared how it was done the previous year. I gradually released that responsibility for planning the graduation and then monitored progress through regularly scheduled meetings.

It Won't Get Done in a Timely Manner

The second reason we fear delegation is that we fear the task won't get done in a timely manner. The strategies that I'm going to share here are also going to help you with conquer the first fear. Using my example above, the first thing I needed to do was to establish a timeline. Then I had to share the timeline and backward map to it. Let me just show you what that looks like. As I gradually released the responsibility for kindergarten graduation to my Family Services Coordinator, I informed him that graduation was on June 15 which meant that everything needed to be done by June 1. We then backward mapped to the timeline. In our first meeting he needed to come to me with a list all the tasks we needed to complete do to have kindergarten graduation. We looked at what he thought needed to be done and at tasks that I thought needed to be done. We then created benchmarks for each task and scheduled them using our shared calendars. By scheduling the dates of all our meetings, I was able to regularly monitor progress, while also being transparent about the dates when certain tasks had to be accomplished. When we backward mapped to benchmarks, and we were able to complete all tasks before or on schedule. The first time that you delegate a task, you're likely going to be more involved than you will the next time the person completes the task.

The one really big takeaway I want my clients to have is by delegation properly we can better ensure the success of the outcomes. When something goes awry, or you don't get the results you anticipated you need to self-reflect. You need to look at yourself and say, "Okay, what did I do to set that up? Did I set it up properly?" If you determined that you didn't set it up properly then you need to create a plan as to how you will set it up differently next time. If you determine that you set it up properly, and the person isn't following through, then you need to have a conversation to remedy the situation.

I Can Do That Really Quickly and I'm Not Good at Delegating

Another reason people give for not delegating is that they believe they can do the tasks themselves quickly. When leaders do that, they are just taking away from other tasks that only they can and need to do. They're continuing to just add things to their dance card that other people can and should. The last reason people give for not delegating is saying, "I'm not good at delegating." The truth of the matter is the only way you get better at delegating is by doing it. If you follow the strategies in this section you will become more confident in your abilities to delegate and more effective at supporting your team members as they take on new responsibilities.

I coached a leader who held on to things so tightly that most things didn't get done. I learned quickly, within two months of coaching her, that she was not coachable. She wouldn't delegate anything, but then she would complain about things not getting done. When I would push her and ask "Well, where are you in this process?" She would say, "Well, I don't have any time I'm so busy." She would agree that she needed to delegate tasks to others in the organization but then she wouldn't. Delegation is a skill that is going to make you a much better leader because you're going to be able to focus on YOUR work. You're going to be able to grow the people around you.

There are tasks that you are not going to delegate, these things are either personal to you or very specific to your job. For instance, if you give the keynote address at the Back-to-School Event, you're not going to delegate the writing of the address to someone else. If you give a speech at graduation, you're not going to delegate someone telling you what to say.

A really simple way to figure out what should be delegated is when you look at a task, figure out who on the organizational chart can help you with that. Sometimes you're delegating a part of the tasks and maybe not the entire task. I find many leaders who are afraid to delegate can effectively delegate ant get more done by implementing these techniques.

Create your Delegation Blueprint and Delegate with Confidence

As the leader of your school or organization you are always faced with managing many projects at once. To keep everything moving in the right direction you need to create accountability systems to ensure that everyone is following through on their commitments with excellence and in a timely manner. Once you have at system in place and everyone is aware of the system it just becomes "the way we do things."

My clients have learned a technique called Delegation Blueprint that helps hold people accountable because everything has been intentionally defined. The steps in creating a delegation blueprint are clear and actionable.

Step 1: Determine the task you will delegate to a team member.

Step 2: Outline your expectations for what "right" looks like for this task.

Step 3: Meet with team member and share your expectation and timeline for completion. Ask team member to come up with the key deliverables and dates and meet with you to review.

Step 4: At the review meeting list out key deliverables that you both feel are necessary for success. Identify benchmark dates to check progress.

Step 5: Create calendar invitations for each benchmark, deliverable, and final product.

Step 6: Create meeting invitations for the benchmarks and monitor progress.

Step 7: Determine what support you will need as you gradually release this task to the person for the first time.

Step 8: Celebrate when the task is complete

In a perfect world this delegation blueprint would work like a charm but sometimes that isn't the case. Sometimes people fall short or fail to follow through on their commitments. Following this framework will help you catch those issues before the task is mishandled.

Delegation Blueprint for <Name of Organization>

Task to Delegate	Person to Complete and Date of Completion	Leader Expectations	Key Deliverables and Dates	Progress Monitoring Meeting Dates
Ex. Plan Kindergarten Graduation	Family Services Coordinator April 15th	Parents in attendance Caps and Gowns	Order diplomas March 1 Create invitations March 15 Order caps and gowns Feb 15 Create program April 1 Line up photographer May 1 Mail invitations June 1 Graduation June 15th.	Every other Tuesday beginning on February 10th

Holding People Accountable with Grace

I had a staff member who was consistently not following through on the tasks given. We would meet and he would not have completed his tasks. It was as if we had never had the conversation or like I had never given a directive at our previous meeting. I realized that this was a failure on my part. I was not supporting him in the way that he needed to be supported. I was not being explicit in my expectations. I met with all my executive team members in a 1:1 setting each week and I realized that I was not clearly monitoring anyone's progress aside from looking at some notes jotted down in my journal. I created a system that I still use today with the schools and leaders I support. It is a simple three column chart, but it has made all the difference for me and for those I serve. Everyone is busy and at any given time something can take our attention away from what we are supposed to be doing and this resource helps keep everyone's eyes on the ball.

Step 1: Create a shared document of a three-column chart with the following column headings: Date/ Discussion Items/ Follow Up

Step 2: Use this document every time you meet. I prefer to set mine up with the most recent meeting at the top, but some other people prefer in the opposite order.

Step 3: Record discussion items with as much details as necessary.

Step 4: In the follow up column be as explicit as possible as to the tasks each person in the meeting will own between meetings.

Step 5: At the subsequent meeting the first thing you are going to do is go over the next steps column. If a task has not been completed highlight it a certain color based on the person whose responsibilities it is. If more time is needed make a notation of the target date for completion.

Step 6: Repeat the process for all meetings.

This tool helps you hold people accountable with grace because timelines and expectations are clearly outlined and shared each week. If someone does not follow through on his/her commitments, then it is time for a supportive or a directive conversation depending on what you uncover in your discussion. The key to holding people accountable is to provide the supports and scaffolds ahead of time so that they can ONLY be successful. It is to no one's advantage if one of our team members fail. Below is an example of the chart.

Dealing with Difficult People

Occasionally we can implement all of the strategies and yet we still have issues with difficult people. The first step for dealing with a difficult person is usually having a conversation. This is easier said than done sometimes, especially if emotions are high. I recommend following the PAUSED Method for Difficult Conversations.

P: Prepare yourself for the conversation. This does not just mean physically prepare with notes but also mentally prepare for the conversation. You should be controlling when and the how long of the conversation which can only be done when you prepare for it. When I explain this to leaders, I tell them that they need to be the "Alpha." If someone comes in and demands that you meet with them and you drop everyting you are relinquishing control.

I agree that if you are available you should meet with them but try this: *"I can tell this is important to you. Give me one minute to stop into my office and button up this {one thing that I am working on}. I'll be right out to grab you so we can have that conversation."* In so doing you have just given yourself time to calm down your reptilian brain that may be firing, prepare yourself for the conversation, and set the terms of the conversation.

A: Allow the other person to share uninterrupted first. Although you are going to want to interrupt to correct things or respond, DON'T. Simply jot down points the person makes and how you would like to respond.

U: Use data and facts, do not use emotions or feelings. Statements like "I think" or "I feel" should not be used. Rather use, "the data shows" or "based on a review of the situation it suggests" or similar language. This is the time when you can refer to your notes and address their comments. If they try to interrupt you say *"Name, I* *provided you time to discuss your concerns uninterrupted. I am asking that you provide me the same."*

S: Summarize the conversation verbally before it ends. What is your expectation of what will happen after this meeting? What will you do? What do you expect the other party to do? *"I am glad that we were able to address X today. To summarize {this is how we are going to handle it moving forward.}*

E: End the meeting when you feel it is over. You should be the alpha here. Do not allow the conversation to go past the point of being productive. *"Thank you for sharing your concerns, unfortunately I have other commitments that demand my attention now."* You can use this even if you don't have commitments. The commitment can be to yourself to move on from this situation. You can always offer a follow-up meeting. What you are NOT going to do is allow this to continue on ad infinitum.

D: Document the conversation in written form, email or messages in your organization's in house app such as Slack is also appropriate. You are documenting what was discussed in step "S" using a more formal method.

The Trajectory is Yours to Change

In the end, leadership is not just about what you give to others—it's about how you value yourself in the process. Feeling appreciated begins with recognizing your worth and setting the boundaries that honor it. The Leadership

Appreciation Syllabus is your guide to reclaiming control, creating balance, and fostering a sense of fulfillment at work and at home. Remember, when you lead with intention and clarity, you teach others how to treat you. It's time to stop running on empty and start leading with purpose and respect—both for yourself and from those around you.

CHAPTER 5

The Leadership Systems Syllabus

"If I didn't fill my schedule with things I felt were important, other people would fill my schedule with things they felt were important."

—Melinda Gates.

There is nothing more frustrating in leadership than having to complete a task and not knowing where to begin. Sadly, many organizations rely on institutional knowledge and don't create repeatable systems. When this happens, leaders are constantly recreating the wheel. The Leadership Systems Syllabus helps leaders reflect on their priorities and the priorities of the organization and ensure there are systems in place. When organizations are effective in creating these systems, everyone can get more done in less time.

Complete the Priority Scorecard

The priorities of the organization and those of the leader are essential for guiding the work. Although we *say* we have certain priorities, the way we act and the amount of time we spend on tasks truly demonstrates our priorities. It is critical that as the leader of your organization and member of your wonderful family that you reflect on, educate others, and live your priorities. For me from the very start my kids were my priority. I was able to go on their field trips, be at their cupcake birthday celebrations, and have lunch with them. I would not have been able to do any of that if they didn't attend the school that I founded and led. There certainly were times when something might have happened when I had to put my responsibilities as the CEO ahead of my role as their mother, but they always knew they were a priority. At work, the students were 100% my priority and the basis of every decision that I made but did I spend my time that way? I'm pretty sure on most days I didn't spend as much time with the students or in their classrooms than I would have liked. Although we *say* we have certain priorities the way we act and the amount of time we spend on tasks truly demonstrates our priorities.

My clients work with me on an activity called a priority scorecard. It gives us data to determine if they truly are honoring their priorities. It provides us a springboard to start a conversation on their current reality and how they may be able to change it. The first thing that my clients do is identify their top three priorities for their families, their organization, and then themselves. The next step is to work on the priority scorecard. To complete the priority scorecard, they need to conduct a three-day time audit. For three days they will record the tasks you do, the amount of time you spend on the tasks, the category the task falls into, if you lead the task or supported the task and who can assist.

At the end of the three days, they sort the categories and calculate how much time they spent leading or supporting in each category. Together, with my client, we look at the data and reflect on the following questions:

1. What is taking up most of my time?

2. Are these tasks my responsibility?

3. If not, why am I involving myself in them?

4. Does this data show that I am living by my priorities?

5. If the data doesn't show that why?

6. Brainstorm what you can do to ensure that what you say are your priorities are the things you spend your valuable time doing.

The information from this exercise helps the leader determine how she is working and how she can further honor the priorities that she has set for herself as a leader and a family member. I recently did this with one of my clients who is the founder and Executive Director of a charter school. After taking the data and reflecting on the patterns we realized that she is spending most of her time on operations which should not be her bucket. We talked about why this was happening and determined that what she really needed was a Director of Operations. We uncovered the situation was circular. The school doesn't have a Director of Operations because the budget can't support it, the budget is built on the number of students they have but they have at least 20 open seats. We set a plan to push recruitment and enrollment to get those seats full. Once the seats are full there will be enough money to hire a Director of Operations who can take over those tasks. If my client and I had not gone through that exercise she wouldn't have realized that the way she was spending her time was not aligned to the priorities that she had for her position. Below is an example of how to set up a time audit using excel so you can easily sort it when you've collected your data.

Honoring Your Priorities

Now that you outlined your priorities above and completed your time audit what actions do you need to take to honor them? Complete the STO/START/ TRY chart below.

What do you need to STOP doing immediately?

What do you need to START doing immediately?

What do you want to TRY?

A Focus on Your Priorities Necessitates Healthy Boundaries

The relationship between your priorities and your boundaries is a critical one. Focusing on your priorities can only happen when you are creating, nurturing, and enforcing healthy boundaries. Now that we've investigated both I would like you to reflect upon the roles they are playing in your daily life.

Are you honoring your priorities every day?

If you are not, why?

Are there boundary issues that are threatening your priorities?

If yes, what are they?

What are you going to do differently to ensure you are honoring your priorities and enforcing healthy boundaries?

When are you going to do this? Set a date and make it happen!

Managing your Time so You Time Doesn't Manage You

Have you ever had a day where you sat down at the end and thought well that was a whirlwind and I got nothing done? Literally, the day went by in a flash, and you couldn't articulate one priority task that was completed. We've all been there. It is on those days that your time managed you. Instead of filling your calendar with priority tasks you allowed everyone else's tasks to create your priorities. Yes, there are days when emergencies happen, and it throws you off, but those days should be few and far between. If you are noticing that you are having those days frequently you need to look at how you are using your calendar, your assistant, and your time.

Protecting your Time

For you to be able to complete ALL the tasks that ONLY for which only you are qualified you must protect your time. I was working with one of my clients, Patty, who showed me her calendar and said, "how do I fix this?" As we went through her calendar it was clear that 90% of the tasks on her calendar were put there by someone else. We looked at a few of the meetings and I asked what is this meeting about? Her answer: I have no idea they just invited me. Patty is an Assistant Superintendent, the only person in the organization who should be inviting her to a mandatory meeting is the Superintendent.

We processed through the calendar, and I helped her understand that she was allowing others to manager her and her time. I asked her how she as using her administrative assistant with scheduling, and she said she wasn't. We created this system to protect her time. The only person who could schedule time on her calendar is her or her administrative assistant. If you are in an organization where calendars are open for everyone to see be sure yours is not open for everyone to schedule. If someone wanted to schedule a meeting with Patty, they would have to contact her administrative assistant. Her administrative assistant would ask three questions:

1. What is the purpose of this meeting?

2. What are the desired outcomes?

3. What role do you want Patty to play in this meeting?

The administrative assistant would take that information and determine next steps.

For example, if the purpose of the meeting is to determine the content for a back-to-school session at one of the 20 district schools, the desired outcome is to create, and Patty's role is to give ideas, this would not get scheduled. We worked together on language the administrative assistant could use.

"Thank you for inviting Patty to this meeting. Unfortunately, she is unable to attend at that time. If there is a particular point you want feedback on, please share the meeting notes with me after and I'll have her look at it and give feedback." or "Patty doesn't attend building level planning sessions. If there is a particular point you want feedback on, please share the meeting notes with me after and I'll have her look at it and give feedback." The first is a softer land and the second really sets the boundary that this is not her area.

The more you attend meetings that you are invited to the more meetings you will be invited to. As leaders we need to set the tone that we are not a team of 1. You have a team that handles different level tasks and if something gets "kicked up to you." You will get involved.

Earlier in the book we went into the important of both boundaries and priorities. Someone once said to me, "Your inbox is filled with what everyone else think are your priorities." BOOM. I never thought of it like that. Yes, yes, yes! I can sort through my inbox and decide, based on my priorities for the day, week, month, year, what I will address and when. A critical role of leadership is monitoring the people and projects in your organization. I hear a lot of leaders say "I don't have time." You do have time; you just have to use it more wisely. We all have the same 24 hours in a day. You can use it to binge Netflix, or you can use it to paint and rearrange your room, you've been taking about it for a year or go through your kids' clothing or begin writing the book you've always wanted to write or go to the gym. I can hear it now, "OK, DMC that sounds great, but you don't know how busy I am." Oh, I know and the only way to make time for things is to make time for things.

When I started the charter school, we were very thin at the top of the organization. We had 194 students, 32 teachers, and two administrators. It seemed like all I was doing the first few months was dealing with behaviors. I was talking to a dear friend of mine, who was actually the first leaders I coached, I was complaining about how I was so busy that I couldn't get into classroom to observe instruction. What happened next was a true full circle moment when the teacher became the student! Toyia said to me "If you don't get into classrooms and make sure the kids are engaging in high quality instruction you won't have a school." She reminded me of what I told her: schedule time to get into classrooms, shut off your radio, tell your team to only contact you if the police, fire department, or ambulance are at the school, they need to handle everything else. So, I stopped feeling sorry for myself, put on my big girl panties, and followed my own advice. From that moment on I ran my calendar and did not let my calendar run me. So I ask you to think about that, are your controlling your calendar and day or are they controlling you?

Setting your Day Up for Success

The day of a female leader can go left very quickly. It is important that you have a plan that honors your work preferences. If we don't run our day our day runs us. We need to look at what we must accomplish and drop those tasks in when we are at our best to conquer them. When I was the CEO of the charter school, I founded I had a consistent morning routine. I would drop my things off in my office and get mentally settled before the students arrived. Once the building was bustling with energy I would do my rounds. I would stop into the offices, classrooms, the cafeteria, and wish everyone a good day and chat people up. I set a personal intention to check-in with everyone before I settled into my day. No matter what happened later in the day, because the unexpected always happened, I had face time with my staff and students. When I returned to the office, I would tackle my emails and any phone messages and take care of those before I got heavy into my work tasks.

When you work best is also an important consideration when you are planning your day. Use the questions below to decide when you will complete certain tasks. For my educators out there, if you are a building leader, I suggest getting into all the classrooms for a morning visit, if you are a district leader I suggest checking in with your central office staff as soon as you arrive and set down your things in your office.

- When do you have the most mental energy?

- When does your energy start to wane?

- When do you like to meet with your executive team?

- What is a good time to visit classrooms/schools?

- When can you block out time for lunch or a mindfulness break?

- What tasks do you need to do every day? Block the time out on your calendar?

- What observations do you need to conduct this week, when? Block time out on your schedule?

- Do you have time sensitive projects that need your focused time? If so, plan for it in your calendar.

Once you have answered these questions plan your days and your week. I suggest going through this bi-weekly to ensure you are continuing to function at your highest, most efficacious level.

Wrapping up Your Day

There is nothing worse than starting your work day unfocused and unsure of what you need to accomplish for the day or week. I coach my clients through a very simple system for planning their next day at the end of the current day. It is a very simple technique that takes about two minutes to complete and pays huge dividends in keeping you organized and on track.

At the end of each day, about 30 minutes before you leave create your "Must Do" and "Can Do" lists for the following day. You can write it on paper or use the task features on your email. Personally, I love checking things off my list. The "Must Dos" are tasks that are time bound and must happen. It could be part of a project or a complete task. Your goal is to be able to check those off your list before you leave for the day. You can book time on your calendar for the next day to be sure you have time set aside to complete the task. The "Can Dos" are tasks that you can drop in if you have a few minutes between responsibilities or are projects that have a longer timeline.

When you enter the following day use this list to plan what gets accomplished for the day. Block time off on your schedule to complete tasks. At the end of the following day check off what was accomplished and create your list for the following day. This running list becomes an artifact of what you have accomplished for the week. Look back at it on Friday and be amazed!

Taking on Large Projects

In education we use a technique called Backward Mapping when we create units of study. The foundation of this technique is "Beginning with the End in Mind." Instead of just going forward and taking steps that we *hope* will result in us achieving the goals, we start with the goals and map out task backwards. This technique is also how leaders can manage big projects.

The best way to manage large projects is to create public action plans and backward map to the final product. When you use these techniques, you are crystal clear on the outcomes, the necessary action steps, and the timeline.

Recently a leader shared with me that she had implemented this technique with a person in her organization who is a global thinker. He has difficulty seeing the steps that lead to the final project. She confided that this has made it difficult for her to work with him and caused frustrations because he often did not meet his deadlines. She reported that this technique worked perfectly. The meeting was focused, results-oriented, and when it was over everyone knew *exactly* what they needed to do before the next check-in meeting because it was laid out on the action plan.

Action Plans are a Must

I'm not going to lie I love me some action plans! When you can brainstorm with your team and get all your best ideas on the table you create an action plan that will yield amazing results. I use a very simple template when action planning. The reason action plans are an effective tool is because you have captured the highest leverage actionable steps that people need to take to achieve the outcomes are captured and listed in one location. Additionally, you have set a time frame by which the work needs to be completed and assigned it to a specific team member. Some of you who are reading this may be thinking *action plans schmaction plans*. Well hear this, they are a game changer and help people meet their goals and help you monitor progress and hold team members (and yourself) accountable. To create an effective action plan, follow the following steps:

Step 1: *Be clear when you define the objective.* Defining an achievable objective is the foundation upon which effective action plans are built. Be sure that you and your team have collaborated and put their best and their next best ideas on the table.

Step 2: *Develop high leverage action steps that will achieve the outcome with less stress.* Once the objective is identified the team should start listing high leverage action steps. Usually there are many steps that can be listed but you and your team want to be laser focused and choose action steps that will give the biggest payoff.

Step 3: *Develop a timeline.* A detailed timeline will ensure that the action plan is effective. There should be a final date by which the objective will be achieved. Additionally, I recommend regular check ins to gauge progress.

Step 4: *Identify who will be responsible for each action step and include a target date for completion.* When the team captures the date by which action steps should be completed, they can also add interim check in dates which provides an added level of support and accountability to team members.

Step 5: *Determine resources the team needs to successfully achieve the objective.* An effective action plan also includes any resources that the team may need to be successful. These can be physical as well as human resources.

Step 6: *Monitor progress and adjust as necessary.* Action plans are great tools, and their implementation needs to be monitored and adjusted as necessary. The length of the project and the number of action steps will determine how often the leader should monitor progress. I recommend it being on every leadership meeting as a check in. It doesn't need to be a big discussion. It can simply be "Does anyone need any help with their action steps? Are we still on track to meet our deadline?" At that time, you can adjust timelines or tasks as necessary. This will also allow you to review and reflect upon the efficacy of the action plan.

Step 7: *Communicate effectively with the team.* Communication should be consistent and effective. Use whatever means your team likes and be clear with your communications.

Step 8: *Celebrate small and big wins.* Celebrating when action steps are completed will keep the team motivated and feel acknowledged.

For action plans to effectively help your team achieve their objectives you and your team need to be realistic. Using weight loss as an example, if we create an action plan lose 100 pounds in 1 week there is no way that would ever be realistic. A person may be able to lose 100 pounds in a few months but certainly not overnight. Team members must also be consistent and committed to the objective and the plan. Effective action plans are monitored, team members provide feedback, and are regularly reviewed and updated as needed. Below is an example of a very simple action plan

Grow Your Team

I firmly believe that the most important job of a leader is to grow more leaders. We need to build a team so that people are ready to step in when others step out. A critical piece of your leadership is your ability to ensure you create a sustainable leadership pipeline that better serves the needs of all your stakeholders. Here is the problem that I've seen repeatedly with the leaders and organizations that I support. Once hired, leaders don't usually get any sort of leadership development opportunities. Sometimes it is because they have thrown themselves into the role and are merely surviving and other times it's because the organization doesn't have a plan in place. When new leaders do receive professional learning it's usually a one-shot deal with no significant job embedded follow up. That common approach doesn't work anymore. Leaders need more than a fly by night PD opportunity.

Leaders can quickly become an island in a stream. They're isolated and don't have a system to address their daily challenges. These leaders can't act quickly or competently and often will look to you for constant guidance and reassurance. A system to support leaders so they stay in their roles and grow into other roles within the organizations is needed.

Using education as an example, every year 17% of principals did not serve the same school two years in a row. 45% of superintendents don't last more than three years, in the largest districts with the highest levels of poverty, about 10% of the districts in the nation, 71% of superintendents didn't last more than three years. These number illustrate how critical it is to create a stable system that grows leaders from within your organization. So, what should you do? You should reassess your leadership development plan, build a strong team and take a route that will ensure you have effective leaders who are able to operate at a high level in challenging educational environments.

The best legacy that I left when I stepped down as the CEO was my school leadership team. I had 11 people who served in a variety of leadership positions. Seven of them served in positions into which they grew over time. When I started a school, it was pretty much just me. As the school began, I realized I needed to empower more people and distribute leadership.

What I had been doing, and what some of you are currently doing, was and is NOT SUSTAINABLE. So, how do you build a great team?

Step 1: Find people who are BETTER than you. Yes, you read that correctly. Figure out what areas of your program where you aren't expert and find someone who is.

Step 2: Empower those who are BETTER than you to take action to support the teachers and staff. Create positions if you need to!

Step 3: Invest in the growth of those people to GROW their leadership.

Step 4: TRUST them to complete their tasks with quality.

Letting Go: Trusting Your Team

One of the biggest mistakes I find that some leaders make is to try to control things too tightly. They simply don't want others to perceive that they don't know something and the answer to that is CONTROL. This strategy will NEVER work. What a leader must do is trust the team. The people in your organization have institutional knowledge and understand how things work, maybe in a way that you do not. You may have heard the phrase "Trust but Verify." I advocate to trust your team until you have reason not to.

You can trust your team while holding your team accountable by following these suggestions.

Step 1: Meet with your people and be clear on your expectations for their position and for them. Be sure that there is CLARITY for both of you.

Step 2: Plan regular meetings with your team members and follow an agenda where your leaders can report out on what they accomplished. Hold them accountable for doing what was discussed and/or assigned to them.

Step 3: Keep notes of your meeting and record what was and not accomplished. Start each meeting with a review of the previous week's tasks to be sure they have been met. If they hadn't been then make a plan to be sure they are.

Step 4: Support your leaders' growth so they can continue to be effective. Give them kudos when they do things that will better the organization.

Step 5: Honor their special skills by ensuring they can exercise them.

Step 6: Show appreciation to your team... ALWAYS.

As you grow your team be mindful that people will need your guidance and support. Figuring out how much support is needed may take time, but it is worth it. As you focus on each leaders' skills and responsibilities you will be growing his/her capacity to take on bigger tasks. Just as a teacher provide scaffolding and gradually releases responsibilities to their students you will do the same with the leaders that you develop.

Get More Done in Less Time

In the everyday pace of work where time is a scarce commodity, female leaders must leverage effective strategies to skillfully manage their tasks. The Pomodoro Technique, a time management method developed by Francesco Cirillo, offers a structured yet flexible approach that can significantly increase productivity, allowing these leaders to accomplish more in less time. The technique is simple to implement. The first step is to choose a task, then you set a timer for 25 minutes, this is known as a 'Pomodoro', work until the timer rings, and then take a 5-minute break. After you've created four work units take a longer break of 15-30 minutes. It is important to follow the intervals because they are specifically designed to maximize focus and prevent burnout. As female leaders we navigate complex responsibilities, often balancing administrative duties, staff and student concerns, and our personal lives. The pressure is immense, and the Pomodoro Technique can be an ally in managing these demands.

Sometimes when I must tackle a large project, I become overwhelmed with the sheer scope of it and can become paralyzed about where to start. The Pomodoro Technique helps in that I don't have to think abut the entire project but can just focus on one task for a finite amount of time. This enables me to be laser focused for 25 minutes and then give my brain a break. That break allows me to reset and refocus on the next task. I can get more accomplished in less time using this technique. Here are some tips to help you maximize the effects.

Blocking off Time: Be sure you are blocking off time that works for you and your energy levels. If you have your best ideas first thing in the morning, then that would be the time do start implementing this method.

Be Flexible: Although there is a prescribed method of time you can be a bit more flexible. If you have completed the task in less than the allotted 25-minut time, then take your break early. It would not make sense to start a new task. Conversely, if you are near the end of your 25-minute block of time and need just a few more minutes to wrap the task up take them.

Minimize Disruptions: When you implement this work flow it would make sense to shut your door, place a sign that indicates you are not to be disturbed, and shut of your phones or notifications. This will help you stay focused during each cycle.

Use it Thoughtfully: Not every task is well suited for this technique. Choose tasks that necessitates focused concentration to complete. The scope of the project will not necessarily dictate its use, the amount of your mental energy will.

For female leaders who are seeking to optimize their time and productivity, the Pomodoro Technique offers a valuable strategy. By fostering focused work periods and regular breaks, it creates a rhythm that enhances concentration and reduces fatigue. By individualizing the technique to your needs and committing to the fidelity of implementation, this method can be a powerful tool for navigating the multifaceted role of educational leadership, fostering not only career success but also work-life harmony.

Create The Organization's Year Task List

Whether you are a new or experienced leader if the organization does not have organized systems around their regular tasks, it will be like the movie Groundhog's Day. You or your team will have to complete a task, and no one will really know the next steps, they may think they know but there are not artifacts. It will be as if this is the first time anyone has ever done it. I work with my clients to create a document called the Yearly Task List. This document has all the important tasks in one location with hyperlinks to the resources needed to successfully complete it.

1. Create a shared excel spreadsheet that captures the date of the event/task, the task, the person responsible, and resources.

   Across the top have a separate column for each person who may have responsibilities, see examples below. This allows for sorting the list.

2. I suggest starting this at the beginning of your year. Schools tend to run their task lists from July 1-June 30th while other organizations track their lists by the calendar year.

3. If this seems like an overwhelming task you can do it in real time. For instance, In August you can say ok what do we have coming up this month and next and write them in. OR

4. You can try to do the entire year ahead of time and then fill gaps as they come up. In the example below

we were able to complete the chart in 3 one-hour sessions. After each session the department chairperson sought feedback from his directors.

5. You can do this as a group or have each individually work on it.

6. Regularly review the tasks together as a team and add any that are missing.

7. Hyperlink any artifacts that will help someone complete the task in subsequent years.

8. Sort the "all tasks" list by date.

9. Copy the "all tasks" sheet for each of the columns you have for responsible parties. Sort each list by one job title, delete all the other data and name it accordingly.

10. Each person now has yearly task list that is individualized to the job responsibilities.

11. Each month review the current and upcoming tasks from the "all tasks" list.

This technique is the gold standard in systematizing your organization. You and your team will no longer be completing things at the last minute or spending hours trying to figure out how to execute tasks.

All tasks listed on the first tab

Example of a sort of the department chairperson's responsibilities only. Replicate this for each member of the team.

Technological Tools to Cut Down on Work Time

There are many technological tools that female leaders can use to cut down on work time. As this book is being written we are just scratching the surface of how AI can help in the daily life of a school or district leader. I used ChatGPT and Otter.ai in the writing of this book which helped me use content I created in other platforms and organize my thought in a cohesive way. AI, just like anything else, is a resource. It provides the user a starting point. Personally, I use what is provided to get my own creative juices flowing and adjust what I like to my voice and my personality. The best way to use AI is to personalize it to you.

Chat GPT: The quality of the output is based on the input so craft your requests with a lot of detail. The more you use Chat GPT the more it gets to know you, your needs, and your style. You can use ChatGPT for a large array of things such as outline speaking points, creating an outline for your parent newsletter, and even crafting a letter to a stakeholder.

OtterAi: I love to use OtterAi to create transcripts of conversations or to dictate information. I find this to be much more accurate than using voice to speech on my phone or in the google suite of products. For this book I transcribed several presentations I had given and cut out parts that I wanted to use. As an educational leader you can use it to transcribe a parent meeting you attended and use information from the transcript in follow up artifacts. You will need to edit it very closely; you can't just copy and paste the information. For those administrators who still script lessons this tool would be a game changer. All you have to do is record using your laptop or phone.

Real Fast Reports: Real Fast Reports can be used with specific input from the user to create high-quality reports. Again, the more detailed the user is with information the better the quality of the output. As with all AI it should not merely be "plug and play" educational leaders should us the output as a guide or a draft of the final product.

Report Genie: Similar to Real Fast Reports, this tool can help your teachers who struggle with writing progress reports or report cards. Using AI to help teachers give accurate and thoughtful feedback in seconds.

Eleven Labs: You know those PD requirements your staff need to check off and can be done by a sit and get method or how to guides for you parents? You can create a presentation deck and this AI voice-over will use exact clone of your voice to speak the content creating an evergreen presentation with ease.

Tome: This AI tool can help you create amazing presentations. The user adds in a few keywords, and will get text, images, and even a layout that optimizes the content.

Pollinations: No more spending hours looking for the perfect image to go along with your parent or staff newsletter. This AI tool is a text to image creator.

Merlin: This resource is an AI plugin that puts ChatGPT into your browser so that you can answer an email with the help of AI. Naturally this may not be one that you use for everyday emails, but it may be worth a try for the odd email that's outside of your zone of comfort.

Writesonic: There were times when I would start at my computer and think "What do I want to write about in this newsletter?" If that has ever been you then this AI tool is for you, it allows you to create articles or emails to share with your stakeholders.

Mapdeduce: This AI tool can be used to summarize any document. The user can upload a PDF and get a summary without having to read the entire document. An additional benefit is that the user can ask questions and the tool will provide answers that it culls from the PDF.

With the growth of AI many of the electronic resources your school already uses have incorporated some form of AI. I would recommend having your organization's IT professional research which AI enhancements have been made and how they can make everyone's lives easier.

Technology can also be used to help manager large projects. Using a shared calendar, a shared presentation or document, and keeping all shared materials updated will serve as a very simple project management tool. If you are a leader of a larger organization such as a school district or a CMO it might behoove you to invest in project management resources like Monday, Smartsheet, or Asana. A simple search of project management tools will help your team determine which tool would best suit your needs. Technology tools can significantly ease the burden of the work for an already overworked female educational leader. When I work with my clients we dive down and determine which tasks are taking up the most of our time and we seek to find resources that will east that burden. AI in general can serve to do this effectively and should not be feared.

Which AI resources can help you in your daily work as a female educational leader? Complete the chart below.

AI Resource	I will use it for	I will use it by (pick a date)

As leaders, our most precious resource is time. Without clear systems, even the most capable leader can become trapped in a cycle of inefficiency, leaving little room for innovation or personal growth. The Leadership Systems Syllabus is not just a tool—it is a mindset shift that prioritizes sustainable success.

When we invest in creating repeatable systems, we reclaim our time and energy, ensuring that our organizations run smoothly even in our absence. These systems empower our teams to thrive, minimize unnecessary stress, and allow us to focus on higher-level priorities that drive impact. Most importantly, they enable us to align with our personal values, making room for harmony between work and home.

Remember, great leadership is not about doing it all—it's about creating environments where others can succeed while you lead with clarity and intention. By embracing and implementing the Leadership Systems Syllabus, you lay the foundation for a legacy that is not only productive but transformative for everyone you influence.

The time is now to stop spinning your wheels and start building the systems that will allow you—and your organization—to achieve more than you ever thought possible. The journey begins with one deliberate step forward, and the results will ripple far beyond what you can see today.

CHAPTER 6

The Wonder Woman Within You—Living the Life You Deserve

"I think realizing that you're not alone, that you are standing with millions of your sisters around the world, is vital."

—Malala Yousafzai

Congratulations, you've made it. The pages of this book have guided you through the journey of unlocking your own superhero potential. You've learned to recognize the Wonder Woman within you—not the perfect, unattainable image that society often pushes, but the resilient, resourceful, and powerful woman who balances career, family, and personal well-being with grace and strength. You've seen that **you are Wonder Woman**, and you can win at work and crush it at home—without sacrificing yourself along the way.

This chapter is a celebration. It's a reminder that you've already begun the transformation. You've equipped yourself with the tools, systems, and mindset needed to create the work-life harmony you deserve. Even more than that, you've embraced a new way of thinking one that allows you to honor your needs, protect your time, and prioritize what truly matters in both your professional and personal life.

What You've Achieved

In the pages leading up to this moment, you've learned:

- **Self-care isn't selfish**: You've realized that investing in yourself is essential. When you take care of your physical, emotional, and mental health, you show up as the best version of yourself for your family, your team, and your community.

- **Boundaries are your armor**: Like Wonder Woman's indestructible bracelets, your boundaries protect your energy and well-being. You've learned to communicate and enforce these boundaries in a way that allows you to focus on what truly matters.

- **Priorities guide your choices**: You've discovered the power of clarity—knowing what to say "yes" to and what to say "no" to. With this newfound focus, you are no longer scattered or overwhelmed by every request or expectation placed on you. You're intentional with your energy.

- **Systems are your secret weapon**: From time blocking to delegation to morning rituals, you've established systems that streamline your days, reduce decision fatigue, and ensure that you are moving forward with purpose and efficiency.

The Real Work-Life Harmony

It's important to acknowledge that work-life harmony, not balance, is the goal. The idea of "balance" can be misleading. Often, life is more like a symphony, with different instruments coming in and out of focus at different times. Harmony is about acknowledging that sometimes your work will demand more of you, and other times your personal life will take center stage. Through this harmony, you learn to navigate those shifts while maintaining alignment with your values and your core priorities.

What matters now is that you have the power to make these shifts intentionally. When work feels overwhelming, you know how to adjust and recalibrate to give yourself space. When family needs your attention, you know how to step back from work without guilt, because you've built a system that allows you to return to your professional commitments with clarity and energy.

You Are Part of a Larger Movement

You're not alone on this journey. The **Sister Leader Movement** is an ever-growing network of women who are dedicated to breaking the mold of burnout and embracing a life that blends purpose, power, and passion. Every time you prioritize yourself, set boundaries, and lead with intentionality, you inspire other women to do the same.

When you model work-life harmony, you show others that it is not just possible but necessary for lasting success.

Your personal transformation is not just for you it's for everyone who looks up to you, from your family to your colleagues to the women you mentor. You are a role model, and as you embrace your true power, you give others permission to do the same. Together, we rise.

Stepping Into Your Power

As you close this book, don't see it as an ending. See it as the beginning of a new chapter where you embrace your inner Wonder Woman every single day. No more waiting for the perfect moment or the ideal conditions. The tools and mindset you've gained are here to propel you forward.

You have what it takes.

You are powerful.

You are capable.

You are worthy of self-care, boundaries, and harmony.

You are Wonder Woman—not because you're perfect, but because you're bold, resilient, and capable of facing challenges head-on.

A Final Thought

Here's the truth: winning at work and crushing it at home isn't about perfection or doing it all. It's about showing up fully as yourself, leading with intention, and creating a life that aligns with your values.

It's about prioritizing what truly matters, not just what seems urgent. It's about giving yourself permission to rest when needed, to say no when necessary, and to celebrate the wins—big and small—along the way.

Now is the time to step forward with confidence, knowing that you've already unlocked the tools you need to build the life you deserve. **The future is yours to create.**

So, Wonder Woman, what will you do next?

What boundaries will you set today?

What systems will you implement tomorrow?

The answers are in your hands, and I have no doubt that you will continue to rise stronger, wiser, and more powerful than ever before.

You are Wonder Woman. Now that you know it the world better watch out.

Book a no pressure discovery call
with Donna Marie

Join my FREE Facebook Group for
Female leaders

ABOUT THE AUTHOR

Dr. Donna Marie Cozine is a leader, author, speaker, and executive coach. After leaving the school she founded, Renaissance Academy Charter School of the Arts in Rochester, New York, she has focused her energies on helping female leaders manage the competing priorities that they face daily. She also works with organizations to create sustainable leadership pipelines that grow leaders from within.

This is Dr. Cozine's third book. Her first Amazon bestselling book, *So You Want to Be a Superintendent? Become the Leader You Were Meant to Be*, outlines her DRIVERS approach to leadership development. Her second

Amazon best-selling book, *Happy Teachers, Joyful Students, Engaged Families A. Guide for Building a School Community That Works,* outlines her SCHOOL JOY method. She is the founder and CEO of DMC Consulting, a company dedicated to serving organizations that want to ensure their leaders and their systems are ready to serve their communities with excellence. She is the founder of the Sister Leader Movement and is committed to helping women achieve their goals and show up for themselves at work and at home.

Dr. Cozine has a Bachelor of Arts degree in social science from Pace University, a Master of Arts degree in social studies education from Fordham University, and a Doctorate in educational administration and supervision from St. John's University.

Dr. Cozine is currently living the dream in Fairport, New York, with her husband Craig, daughter Juliet, son Theo, and her biggest four-legged fan Oliver. Dr. Cozine loves to speak with leaders from around the world to help them reach their goals. To reach Donna Marie, please email her at dmc@consultdmc.com.

THANK YOU

Thank you, my sister leader, for choosing *Winning at Work and Crushing it at Home*. I know time is a commodity you don't have a lot of and am honored you would spend it reading my book. I built this book for female leaders who were like I was. I was overworked, exhausted and on the verge of burn-out. I felt unappreciated and taken advantage of and was sure that I had too much work and never enough time. I am so happy to share my successes and lessons learned with other leaders just like you. Congratulations for making the decision to focus on yourself for a change. May the family that deserves the Best of you no longer have to settle for the REST of you.

After twenty-seven years in education, I shifted from leading organizations to supporting leaders just like you. I believe the true work of leaders is to grow more leaders to take over. I am energized by the work that I do coaching leaders and supporting their teams. If I can be of service to you, please feel free to email me at dmc@consultdmc.com or visit my website to learn about me at consultdmc.com.

Keep leading, keep learning, and keep loving your community! You are a blessing to all those you serve, and I appreciate you.

In friendship, love, sisterhood, and leadership,

Made in the USA
Columbia, SC
31 January 2025

52508318R00070